Small Change

SMALL CHANGE

A Film Novel

François Truffaut

Translated by Anselm Hollo

GROVE PRESS, INC., NEW YORK

ISBN: 0-394-17921-8
Grove Press ISBN: 0-8021-4037-8

Library of Congress Catalog Card Number: 76-44660

First Black Cat Edition 1976
First Printing

Distributed by Random House, Inc., New York

GROVE PRESS, INC., 196 West Houston Street,
New York, N.Y. 10014

For Suzanne

"Children have a way of making me go crazy.
I adore them and I'm a fool."

VICTOR HUGO

Contents

Introduction

For many years I have been interested in true stories about childhood: newspaper clippings, stories by friends, my own memories, all feed my curiosity. *Small Change* was going to be the title of a collection of short stories, which I decided to abandon in order to turn it into a screenplay. To avoid making an episodic film, I have interwoven the action and the characters of those stories and arrived at a form of collective chronicle.

The events of *Small Change* take place in Thiers during the last month of the school year, reaching their climax in August in a summer camp.

Small Change presents about ten youngsters, boys and girls, whose adventures illustrated—from the first feeding bottle to the first loving kiss—the different stages of passage from early childhood to adolescence.

The children, all of whom were newcomers to the movies, were recruited in Paris, Clermont-Ferrand, and Thiers. The parts of adults, parents and teachers, were given to little-known actors, as the true star of a film about children has to be childhood itself.

More than two hundred children's faces appear in the course of this story: a class of thirty-five students, another of twenty-five, a nursery with forty babies, and finally a summer camp with sixty boys and an equal number of girls.

As it is not easy to give a brief description of a collective film, I am going to summon to my aid three artists whom I admire.

Victor Hugo, in his *Art of Being a Grandfather*, Charles Trenet, in the course of two hundred and fifty popular songs of an admirably even quality, and Ernst Lubitsch, indulgent and malicious at once—I see them as three poets who have succeeded in retaining the spirit of childhood.

> Children have a way of making me go crazy.
> I adore them and I am a fool.
>
> VICTOR HUGO
>
> Children are bored on Sundays,
> Sundays children are bored.
>
> CHARLES TRENET
>
> An occasion to laugh is never to be despised.
>
> ERNST LUBITSCH

Those three quotations have been our guides, Suzanne Schiffman's and mine, in the development of *Small Change*, in the choice of episodes and ways of dealing with them. It was a matter of making the audience laugh, not at the children but with them, nor at the expense of the adults either, but with them; thus we had to look for a delicate balance between gravity and humor.

Sylvie has misbehaved and cannot come to the restaurant; Richard lends his haircut money to two friends; Oscar refuses to talk and prefers to express himself by whistling; Bruno does not want to recite his lines "with the proper inflections"; Gregory falls out of a high window; Patrick falls in love with his buddy's mother; Julien is mistreated at home; Martine experiences her first kiss at summer camp.

Obviously the web of *Small Change* is woven out of small events, but let us remember that nothing is "small" in the world of childhood.

Children see the world of adults as the world of impunity, the one in which everything is permitted. An adult can tell his friends with a smile how he happened to total his automobile by running it into a plane tree; on the other hand, a child who breaks a plate while drying the dishes thinks it has committed a crime, as it does not make a distinction between an accident and an offense.

Tossed about between their need for protection and their need for independence, children often have to endure adult caprices, and they have to defend themselves against them, to harden themselves. I stress the distinction: not to grow hard, but hard enough to stand it.

That is what Suzanne Schiffman and I want to express in *Small Change,* while obviously trying to avoid bombast and solemnity. Some of our episodes are funny, others serious, some are sheer fantasy, while others have been culled directly from grim media reports. Together they should animate the notion that childhood is often perilous but that it is also full of grace and that it has a thick skin. The child invents life; it runs into things, but at the same time it develops all its powers of resistance.

Finally, and this is obviously the raison d'être of the film, I never grow tired of making movies with children. Anything a child does on the screen it seems to be doing for the first time, and that is what gives such great value to film used to present young faces in the process of transformation.

February 1976   FRANÇOIS TRUFFAUT

I

The Exact Center
of France

A square, at the intersection of a national highway and a county road. In the middle of the square, a small monument. It is a truncated column on a base. The inscription carved into the stone reads: THIS IS THE EXACT CENTER OF FRANCE.

One of the corners of the square is taken up by a blue building which serves simultaneously as a dry goods, candy, and stationery store, as is often the case in villages.

Lettered on the display window, the store's name: *At the Center of France*. Holding a postcard in her hand, a twelve-year-old girl comes out of the store; she is blonde and wears a red-and-white-checked Vichy dress. Briskly she walks over to the middle of the square and stops in front of the monument. On the back of the postcard, which depicts precisely that column, she writes:

My dear Raoul,
     I am traveling with my father, and we have just stopped in Bruère-Allichamps, which is exactly the center of France. For the first time, I'll be

spending my vacation in a summer camp. I hope it
will be a co-ed camp.

    Love from your Cousin,

Martine

Then quickly Martine slips the card into the
mailbox, and it is on its way to Thiers.

It is beautiful weather in Thiers. The town is
like an encrustation on one of the hillsides of the
Massif Central. All the streets are steep, some of
them being actual stairways of stone. The children
are everywhere, charging down the road from the
railroad station, up and down the streets of the old
town, across the Roman bridge in the Moutiers
quarter; as soon as a dozen of them vanishes round
one street corner, eight others burst out of a side
street. As in cartoons, there is always a little
straggler bouncing along behind all the others.

It is really beautiful weather. Is it possible to
shut oneself up inside four walls on such a day?
The answer unfortunately is yes: here we are at the
public school of Thiers, in the lower division
classroom.

Steadily the male teacher's voice is heard dictating a geography lesson:

"The soil is granitic and impermeable, and there
are numerous streams, rivers, and lakes . . ."

The postcard from Bruère-Allichamps sits stuck
in a groove of Raoul's desk. Raoul is contemplating
it with fascination.

M. Richet has noticed this and interrupts the
dictation.

"Raoul Briquet, you're not writing; bring me
what you've got there. Come on, hurry up!"

Briquet rises, hanging his head low, and walks

16

over to give the teacher the corpus delicti. The teacher takes the card, looks at it, smiles.

"Well, well, I know that little hamlet. That's Bruère-Allichamps!"

Reassured, Raoul Briquet raises his head and stands in front of the blackboard, listening to the young teacher's discourse:

"Let me explain this to you: it's a little town, or rather, a village, situated in the exact center of France. So they put up a little monument, and here it is on this card. Take a look."

M. Richet holds up the card in front of the class, at arm's length. The pupils move about, trying to see it better.

M. Richet turns the card over, finds himself reading the message without having intended to do so. His smile grows wider.

"Well, this is amusing. I'll copy out the address exactly the way it's written on this card, so you can all see it."

In large letters the teacher writes out the address, at the same time reading it in a loud voice:

Raoul Briquet
Béranger Apartments
Thiers
Puy-de-Dôme
France
Europe
The Universe

The chalk breaks on the final word, which makes the kids burst out laughing. M. Richet turns around:

"Is there anyone in this class who has been to Bruère-Allichamps?"

One boy raises his hand. The teacher motions

him to come forward:

"Laurent Riffle, come up and tell us."

Laurent Riffle, who now takes Raoul's place in front of the blackboard, is a little blond fellow with blue eyes and a perennial smile.

"I've been to Bruère-Allichamps because my daddy is a hairdresser and they had this reunion there for all the hairdressers."

M. Richet cuts in:

"A hairdressers' *convention* . . ."

The class is listening with interest, but laughter breaks out again as Laurent concludes:

"And they had this great meal, they went on eating all afternoon. But I got bored, so I went and took a walk in the park."

It becomes obvious that Laurent has nothing further to relate about his visit to the "center of France," and M. Richet turns back to the class:

"Who else has been to Bruère-Allichamps?"

A small brown-haired boy with lively, restless eyes stands up in the back of the classroom.

"Me, sir!"

It is Mathieu Deluca; his kid brother, Franck, eight years old, sits in the row in front of him because M. Richet's class has two sections—the first-year and second-year elementary courses.

"You have, Mathieu? Well, tell us a little about what it's like there."

"I haven't been there, sir."

"So you're just showing off, eh? What did you raise your hand for?"

"Because it says there on the blackboard 'Thiers, Puy-de-Dôme,' and nowadays it should say 'Thiers 63300!' "

Mathieu appears quite pleased with this demonstration of his knowledge.

The teacher yields.

"Oh, well, at least you know the zip code."

There is a knock on the classroom door; its upper half has two panes of the thick and semiopaque glass known as cathedral glass.

M. Richet goes to open it. In the hallway one can now see the young woman who knocked. She has soft-curled brown hair, wears it quite short, and her straight-cut smock does not entirely conceal her advanced stage of pregnancy. She looks shy, does not dare to come any closer.

The pupils are about to rise to their feet, but M. Richet stops them:

"No, no, stay in your seats."

Then, in a low voice, to the young woman:

"Well, Lydie, what is it?"

"You forgot to give me the keys this morning, and now the movers are waiting. They can't start moving the furniture."

While Richet is going through the pockets of his jacket, which is hanging on a coat-tree close to the door, Lydie cannot restrain herself from casting a few curious glances into the classroom. The curiosity is entirely mutual, and the pupils stare back at the young woman.

Having found the keys, the teacher walks back to her.

Lydie puts the keys in her purse; her husband bends to kiss her, hesitates for a moment, glances at the class, and decides to close the door behind him. Laughing and nudging each other, the kids see the shadow play through the cathedral glass: the teacher kissing his wife.

In the schoolyard the children are yelling and shoving each other. It is recess.

Mathieu sits in a corner of the yard, surrounded by a few other young scamps, reciting his version of a counting rhyme:

> *Tu m'as déja vu, tête de morue?*
> *Tu me reverras, tête de rat*
> *Sur mon balcon, tête de con*
> *Chez moi, tête de chamois*
> *Rue Marbeuf, tête de boeuf*
> *Rue Marceau, tête de veau!* *

Recess is over; time to go back to work.

* You have seen me already, you codfish head?
  You'll see me again, rat's head
  On my balcony, shithead
  At my place, head of a chamois
  Rue Marbeuf, head of a steer
  Rue Marceau, head of a calf!

II

Harpagon's Tirade

Now we are in the upper division classroom. Through the still-open door we see M. Richet ascending the stairs, followed by his pupils. Mlle Petit's pupils are already in their seats, and she stands in front of the blackboard, writing and reading what she has written in a loud voice:

"*The Miser*, by Molière."

A latecomer appears in the door. He closes it softly behind him and tries to reach his seat on tiptoe, hoping to avoid a reprimand.

But without turning, as if she had eyes in the back of her head, Mlle Petit remarks drily:

"Well, well, Fougerie, late as ever?"

And she picks up again where she left off reading what she has written on the blackboard:

"Harpagon's tirade, act 4, scene 7. Up to line 15."

Fougerie has reached his desk. He sits down, opens his schoolbag, takes out his copy of *The Miser*, a small book, and opens it to the page indicated.

Mlle Petit proceeds to the interrogation period.

"Desmouceaux, let's hear *The Miser*."

"I haven't got it yet, mademoiselle."

"What do you mean, you haven't got it yet? Come here!"

Desmouceaux, twelve years old, a good alert face under well-combed blond hair, walks over to the teacher and with a carefree air repeats:

"I haven't learned it yet, mademoiselle."

"But that's ridiculous!"

She turns to the classroom at large:

"I did give the assignment, didn't I?"

The entire class responds affirmatively, despite Desmouceaux's dumb show negating it.

"You have learned *The Miser*, all of you?"

And the chorus of pupils responds once again:

"Yes, mademoiselle."

Desmouceaux introduces a diversionary tactic:

"I guess I wasn't here, I don't even have the text!"

Some voices are raised in the classroom in support of Desmouceaux, in a vague murmur: "That's right, he was sick." Mlle Petit takes a pamphlet from her desk and gives it to the boy:

"You have five minutes. Now listen to the others, and then I'll check you on it."

The recitation begins. Mlle Petit does not appear to be too happy with the result: even those who have managed to memorize the speech well are reciting it mechanically without any expression at all. Chantal Petit seems very irritated.

In the empty schoolyard one can hear the hopeless litany of successive Harpagons sounding like an amateur talent show on the radio:

> *Catch the thief, catch the thief*
> *The assassin, the murderer*
> *Mercy, merciful Heaven!*
> *I am lost, I have been murdered!*

In the middle of the deserted yard stands a small, scowling brown-haired boy. He is looking around as if to familiarize himself with his surroundings, clutching under one arm a schoolbag that looks none too appetizing. The school janitor, M. Touly, has seen him and approaches.

"What are you doing here, my boy? You don't go here, do you?"

The boy does not answer.

"How did you get here? Did someone drop you off? I shouldn't think it was a helicopter that dropped you off here, in the middle of the yard!"

Still no answer.

"Are you deaf, or dumb?"

Without a word, the boy pulls out a piece of paper from his cardboard bag and hands it to the janitor, who unfolds it and reads it.

"I see, this is from the mayor's office. They're sending us new ones *now*, in the middle of June? Well! Let's go see the principal."

Touly leads the new boy over to the principal's office, which is in the far corner of the yard. He knocks on the door: no answer.

"The principal isn't here. Are you sure they didn't give you some other papers, too, at the mayor's office?"

The janitor looks at the boy, tries to guess his age, makes up his mind:

"We'll go see M. Richet."

He leads the way, and they disappear into the school building.

In Chantal Petit's classroom it is Desmouceaux's turn to recite from *The Miser*. He starts out well, but after a few lines he comes to a halt, raising his eyes heavenward as if to gain inspiration there.

Mlle Petit intervenes:

"You see, that's not bad at all for five minutes' study. But if you had put in some time yesterday, you'd know a little more of it now. All right, you can sit down . . . Rouillard, let's hear from you."

Bruno Rouillard must be at least thirteen and a half years old, he seems more mature than the other pupils, but not too excited about reciting the tirade from *The Miser*. He gets up slowly and blunders through the text as if he did not understand one word of it. Mlle Petit is very annoyed; she makes him recite it again, and a third time, but it does not improve in the least. She even declaims the text herself to make him understand what it is that she wants. To no avail. Yet Mlle Petit is not ready to let go of her victim.

"Well, maybe you're feeling stubborn, but so am I. Never mind, we have all morning, all day . . . But you *are* going to do it right. Well, start over. It isn't all that difficult:

> *Catch the thief, catch the thief*
> *The assassin, the murderer . . .*

Rouillard resumes his recitation without enthusiasm and finds himself happily interrupted by the arrival of M. Richet and the new boy. M. Richet introduces the boy to Mlle Petit:

"Excuse me, Mlle Petit, this is Julien Leclou. He's a new student, but he is too old for my division, so I guess he should come here."

Mlle Petit points to a desk at the rear of the classroom:

"Over there's an empty seat for you. Go and sit down."

Julien Leclou walks through the classroom, followed by curious stares. He himself does not even look at the other pupils. While he gets settled, the two teachers continue their low-voiced conversation.

"Well, I'm surprised—surely the principal would have told me? I'm sure it's a mistake."

"I just don't know, the janitor just brought him to me, with a note from the mayor's office . . ."

Leclou sits down in the last row, right behind Rouillard, who turns around to look at him and asks him:

"Where do you live?"

"Over by Les Mureaux."

"There aren't any houses there—there's only factories."

"Sure there are houses. I live there," replies the new boy with a shrug.

The teachers have decided to go and clarify matters with the principal; they leave the classroom after Mlle Petit has appointed one of the pupils to be "in charge of the class."

The door has hardly closed behind them when Bruno Rouillard bounds out of his seat, runs over to the door to make sure that the teachers are gone, and grandiosely announces to the entire class:

"Now I'm going to show you how to really do Harpagon!"

And now that the teacher is not there and it is merely a question of amusing his classmates, Rouillard gives free rein to his intuition and gives a dazzling interpretation of Harpagon's character. He slouches through the aisles, bending and

writing and declaiming, giving a performance worthy of Charles Dullin!

> *Catch the thief, catch the thief*
> *The assassin, the murderer*
> *Mercy, merciful Heaven!*
> *I am lost, I have been murdered!*
> *They've cut my throat, they've taken my money.*
> *Who could it be? Where has he gone?*
> *Where is he? Where is he hiding?*

Bruno runs around the room, gesticulating, shouting, weeping, to the greatest delight of his classmates.

While crossing the schoolyard M. Richet and Mlle Petit hear the sounds of Rouillard's performance through the open window. M. Richet is amazed:

"They're really doing great in there. Are you teaching them a drama course?"

Mlle Petit prefers not to admit her own astonishment:

"Well, yes. I have some pretty good ones in the class."

The school principal is back in his office, and the two teachers want to know what to do about that strange new recruit, Julien Leclou.

The principal, M. Berbert, does not waste words:

"That new little fellow? He'll be in Mlle Petit's class. He's been sent to us by the mayor's office, they ask us to keep him here until the end of the year, and . . . well, between us I think he is a social case . . ."

III

Julien, Patrick, and Mme Riffle

In the lower part of town in the middle of a kind of wasteland stands an isolated wooden shack, blackish against a background of vivid greenery, in definite contrast with its surroundings. We are in the quarter of Les Mureaux ("The Walls").

And here is the "new boy," Julien Leclou, scrambling up a ramshackle wooden stairway, heading for the isolated shack. Patrick Desmouceaux, on his way home from school, has stopped for a moment in order to watch him. Patrick is obviously intrigued—by the neighborhood, by Julien's being there. Patrick could have sworn that no one lived in that shack.

Yet Julien arrives in front of it and tries to enter, but the door seems to be locked. He goes and picks up an old ladder and, as if this were the most normal thing in the world, leans it against the front of the shack, climbs up, and disappears through the fanlight window that stands ajar on the second floor.

Patrick resumes his walk home; since he lives alone with his paralytic father, he takes care of the shopping on the way.

When he gets home, his father points out to him

that he has forgotten to take the shopping list along that morning. No matter; even without the list Patrick has remembered everything, and he unloads the bag in the kitchen—oil, sugar, bread, and apples.

Confined to his wheelchair behind a metal desk on which an open book is lying, M. Desmouceaux is still a young-looking man, and his fairly massive shape brings to mind the familiar silhouette of the paralytic detective hero of the American television series *Ironside*.

In another corner of Thiers one of M. Richet's students, Richard Golfier, is likewise walking home from school.

In front of a grocery store he passes a young woman carrying a double load: on one arm she holds her twenty-one-month-old son, Gregory, while the other is encumbered by a shopping basket. Nicole Felix knows Richard well, they live in the same housing complex, and she entrusts the infant to him, asking him to take Gregory home. She still has some more shopping to do, and Gregory is getting heavy. Without much ado Richard starts leading him toward the apartment block Jean-Zay Apartments.

Arriving in front of their door, Richard and Gregory, one trailing after the other, are surprised to see a moving van and pieces of furniture standing on the sidewalk. When they arrive in the third-floor hall, the mystery is solved; it is the teacher himself, Jean-François Richet, who is moving into an apartment on the same floor that Richard lives on.

Jean-François and Lydie Richet meet young Gregory for the first time.

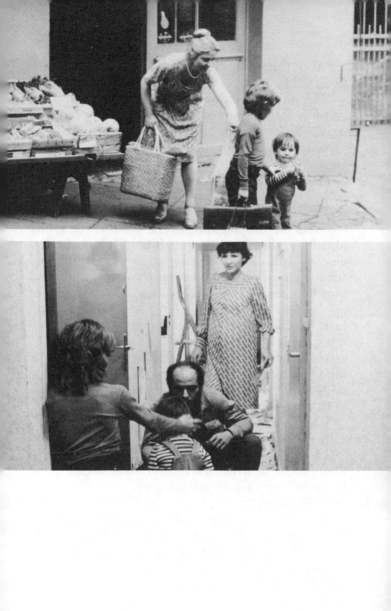

"And this little fellow, is he your brother?" Lydie asks.

"No, he just lives here too, up on the ninth floor, and his mother asked me to take him home," replies Richard, very proud of his mission.

And night falls on the town.

The following morning, still intrigued by what he has seen the previous afternoon, Patrick on his way to school casts a glance at the board shack standing in the middle of the wasteland. Quite obviously the shack is inhabited: Julien Leclou emerges from it. As always, he is wearing his old striped jersey, blue and white, too large; under his arm he carries his old schoolbag, which does not appear very heavy. After a few meters Julien stops, feels his bag, seems to reflect a moment, and then retraces his steps.

The shack door must have been closed from the inside, because Julien is just as unable to open it as he was the day before. He starts knocking on it until a rather unfriendly female voice calls out:

"Well, what is it now?"

"I forgot my schoolbooks."

The little window above the door on the first floor opens a little wider and two books come flying out to crash at Julien's feet.

"There they are!"

Julien picks up the books, and only after some twenty steps and having made sure that no one in the shack can see him anymore, he decides to open his bag and slip the books inside, at the same time revealing what it is he wants to hide—pieces of a broken plate.

On the street leading to the school Julien has stopped to talk to a young apprentice in blue overalls, hardly older than himself, who is busy repairing his bicycle.

"Hi. Is your bike broken?"

"No, no. It just slipped the chain."

The apprentice turns the bike over onto its wheels and starts walking, accompanied by Julien, who uses the opportunity to quiz him.

"Did you watch TV last night?"

"Yeah, sure, I did."

"What was on?"

"An American serial, *Colombo*."

"What happened?"

"Oh, it's about this sabotage job on a racing car ..."

It is obvious that Julien's questioning of the young workingman is designed to elicit, word for word, all the details of the installment, which he evidently has not seen.

Walking on, Julien stops at a street corner in front of a sewer opening and furtively rids himself of the shattered plate he has been carrying in his bag. Striking bottom, the fragments break once again, with a noise multiplied by the echo in the sewer.

On the steps of the church, not far from school, a few boys have stopped to discuss their allowances: how much each one gets and what he does with it ... Then there is another group, of smaller children, among them Sylvie, a ravishing little blonde with huge eyes. Franck Deluca, Mathieu's younger brother, is ready to do anything to hold her attention. His courtship is conducted in an aggressive manner:

"I heard they found you in a garbage can."

Sylvie, a logically-minded girl, replies calmly:

"That isn't true. I was born in Toulon."

Franck insists:

"Well, then they found you in a garbage can in Toulon."

But there goes the school bell—time to go, and they all get up, though none too fast.

In front of the entrance to the schoolyard little Laurent Riffle has a lot of trouble trying to get rid of his mother, who has walked him there. She asks him:

"Now, you haven't forgotten anything?"

"No, no, no. All right, Mama, why don't you go now?"

"Listen, why don't you let me take you to the classroom!"

"No, go back home now."

"Why don't you want me to pay a visit to your school? You know I like to . . ."

"No, no!"

"Well then, Laurent, at least say goodbye . . . can I give you a kiss?"

Mme Riffle, a tall, beautiful, young blonde woman, seems amused by her son's embarrassment and gives him a long kiss and hug.

That kiss, reluctantly received by Laurent, Patrick Desmouceaux might not have refused at all. He stands there, motionless, lost in admiration of the beautiful Mme Riffle, then greets her deferentially as she walks by, and stares after her as long as he can see her.

In the schoolyard Julien has joined a group that is debating last night's installment of *Colombo*. Listening to Julien's detailed description of the sabotaging of the racing car, no one would suspect that he does not have a television set at home.

A little farther away, young Golfier sits perched

on Mathieu Deluca's shoulders and observes, by means of a huge set of binoculars, something Mathieu points out to him, saying in a dreamy murmur:

"I swear . . . incredibly beautiful, isn't it! I've never seen anything as gorgeous."

The object of the two boys' attention is a window in a neighboring building. Through the glass one can see a ravishing brunette, naked, happily engaged in washing herself.

The show is interrupted by the janitor, M. Touly:

"What are you doing with that thing?"

"Well, they're my dad's binoculars," says Richard Golfier in his customary laconic manner.

"That may be so, but you're not supposed to bring them to school. You're supposed to leave them at home," M. Touly states, walking off.

At the other end of the yard a number of boys are engaged in boisterous horseplay. The janitor gently approaches Julien, who sits daydreaming all by himself under the rain roof of the yard.

"What are you doing there, Leclou, aren't you playing with the others?"

"That's all right, that's all right," says Julien, who does not like anyone to take interest in him.

Finally the yard empties, the classrooms fill, it is time for serious matters.

IV

Patrick Does Battle with the Clock

We are in the big boys' classroom. It is late afternoon. Only ten minutes to go, thinks Patrick Desmouceaux, staring at the clock in the schoolyard, visible through the open window.

Mlle Petit, however, has decided to make her pupils work up to the very last minute.

She writes on the blackboard: "Review of important dates, from the fifteenth to the eighteenth century."

Then, turning toward the class:

"Phalippou! 1572?"

"The massacre of Saint Bartholomew's Day."

"1610?"

"Death of Henri IV."

"1648?"

"Treaty of Westphalia. The Alsace became French."

He has done well, Phalippou has, and on the big clock the hand has moved to 4:24.

Patrick experiences a moment of suspense before Mlle Petit goes on:

"Keraghel! 1685?"

"Louis XIV rescinds the Edict of Nantes."

"1763?"

"Treaty of Paris, loss of India and Canada."

The minute hand advances another minute. It is 4:26 on the dot. Patrick wonders if he is the only one who is worrying: the others look like they knew everything.

"Leclou!"

Well, that one does not seem a bit worried. He is, quite simply, asleep. But Mlle Petit does not seem to appreciate it.

"Leclou! Sorry to wake you up. You look positively haggard. I bet you don't know what 'haggard' means, do you?"

As a matter of fact, Leclou does not seem to give a damn. But Mlle Petit never leaves a train of thought unfinished:

"When you look haggard, you look *lost!* Exactly the way you look, right now. Well, let us take someone else . . ."

The time on the great clock is now 4:28.

It would really be stupid to be caught out now, Patrick thinks; he is holding his breath—

"Jalla! 1492?"

Patrick's hopes soar.

"Er . . . Christopher Columbus discovers America."

"1515?"

Jalla dries up. Luckily the boy next to him whispers, "François I wins at Marignano," and he thinks this will save him, but Mlle Petit interrupts him instantly:

"Yes, that's all right, but you just heard it."

4:29. Only a minute longer, and I'll be all right . . .

"Desmouceaux! 1685?"

Right, it's all over! Patrick remains in his seat, his

eyes riveted to the big clock, determined to play for time.

"Come on, Desmouceaux, do you hear me?"

Patrick has decided to remain seated, staring at the clock.

"Desmouceaux, will you get up, please."

He gets up, but without shifting his stare from that damned minute hand that refuses to move down . . .

"Desmouceaux, *this* is where things are happening now! Look at me, do you hear me? Look at me."

Quite impossible that it isn't half-past already. After all, one minute consists of only sixty seconds. He just has to hold on a little longer.

"But for heaven's sake, Desmouceaux, are you deaf or something? Haven't you heard my question?"

Well, someone has heard Desmouceaux's mute prayer. The long hand jerks down to the half-past mark, and he is saved by the classroom bell.

Looking hypocritically regretful while feeling genuine joy, Patrick looks at Mlle Petit, raises his arms heavenward in a gesture of "what can you do," and sets off at a gallop with his mates, far away from the classroom, far from all of it.

V

Julien's Strange House

Sitting on the bottom step of the staircase leading to his strange house, Julien has his nose in a book.

Patrick, driven by curiosity, has walked over to him, but pretends surprise at finding him there.

"What are you doing?"

Julien answers, rather morosely:

"I'm learning my assignment for tomorrow."

Julien sees quite clearly that Patrick is more interested in the shack, and that does not please him too much.

"What are you staring at? There's no one home, and I forgot my key."

In order to create a distraction, he holds out his book to Patrick:

"Here, why don't you check me?"

Patrick sits down next to Julien and takes the book. Julien proceeds:

"All right, here goes. The metallurgical industry plays a very great role in the economy of France, as it employs over a million people. Its . . ."

As he is hesitating, Patrick prompts:

"Its place . . ."

"Its place . . ."

"is one of honor . . ."

But Julien takes the book back.

"Oh, I don't give a shit . . . Enough of that."

Their conversation is vehemently interrupted by a choleric voice emanating from the shack that Julien has claimed to be empty.

"Julien, for God's sake!"

Julien jumps up and tells Patrick in a low voice:

"Hurry up, get out of here! Don't stay here."

And he starts hurrying toward the house, still gesturing to Patrick to leave.

Patrick rushes down the stairs, but he can still hear the termagant voice screeching:

"What the hell are you up to? Come here immediately!"

Patrick walks away, thinking, *What a strange house, strange Julien, strange parents!*

VI

Gregory Goes Boom

Still the same day. Nicole Felix has done her shopping, accompanied by Gregory who is grumbling because he is tired of walking. Arriving in the entrance hall of her apartment building, she is disappointed to find that the elevator is once again out of order.

She starts climbing the stairs, she lives on the ninth floor, and encourages Gregory to follow her.

At first he is reluctant, because he does not like staircases at all; but then, as he has been given the loaf of bread to carry, that mission elates him, and he starts leading the way up the steps. When they get to the third floor, he charges into the Richets' apartment through the open door.

His mother calls to him from the landing:

"Gregory, don't bother the lady; Gregory, that isn't our place."

But since he does not respond, Nicole finds herself obliged to follow him into the apartment, which is still in a state of chaos—pieces of furniture piled on top of each other, wrapping paper, stacks of books, toolboxes—a veritable paradise for Gregory, who starts rummaging around with great gusto.

Nicole is quite embarrassed as Lydie Richet appears.

"Oh, I'm so sorry, the door was open, and he just ran in . . . Gregory, come on now."

But Lydie reassures her immediately:

"But I know Gregory. We met yesterday, and he's already been here. My husband thinks he is a very bright little boy. Perhaps he'll have him in his class one day."

It is obvious that Lydie, who must have been sorting things out, really welcomes the unexpected interruption. She goes on:

"I'm dying of thirst—would you like to have something to drink?"

"Yes, please, if it's no trouble."

The two women sit down and launch into a friendly chat over a glass of wine. They become so engrossed in their conversation—to tell the truth, Gregory's mother does most of the talking—that the infant, left to his own devices, uses the opportunity to empty out the contents of his mother's shopping bag; observing that no one is paying attention, he carefully proceeds to open a couple of packages of noodles, letting them fall upon the floor like rain.

If Gregory is having a good time, the two young women are amusing themselves too, and Mme Felix cheerfully concludes her story:

" . . . three months later he pulled that classical number on me, you know—'I'm going out to get some matches.' I never saw him again, that's for sure. But I've really been all right, with little Gregory . . . And then about two weeks ago—I'd like you to keep this to yourself, you know, I know I can trust you—there was this little advertisement that intrigued me: a single man . . . who is looking for someone . . . he loves children. Well, it's the Great Unknown!"

"And have you met him?"

"No. I wrote, he answered, and we agreed to meet on Sunday, to get acquainted."

"Well, then . . ."

"He'll be carrying *La Montagne*, you know, the newspaper, and I'll also be carrying one."

"Well then, here's to the stranger!" says Lydie, smiling, raising her glass.

"That's right, to the stranger!" says Mme Felix and raises hers.

At this point the two chatterboxes remember the child, and turning around they are stunned by the sight of a cheerful Gregory sitting in the midst of noodles and gateaux, which he has unwrapped and spread out on the floor.

It is time to continue on the laborious journey up to the ninth floor. Gregory and his mother leave and arrive there. The young woman unlocks the door to her apartment, and after he has been relieved of the loaf of bread which he has been carrying like a flag, the boy goes to his room to play with the cat.

Mme Felix proceeds to stow away her shopping in the kitchen; then she notices that she does not have her change purse. She tries to interrogate the youngster, one never knows, but Gregory seems very positive: no, he has not seen the purse . . . no, he hasn't hidden it anywhere . . . no, he hasn't lost it—the noes and the yeses start intermingling, there is no way Nicole can find out the truth.

The young woman tells her son to take care and goes back downstairs to see if she has not dropped the purse somewhere on the way.

Gregory, by himself now, leaves his toys and

picks up his kitten and starts walking round the apartment with it. Finally he enters the kitchen. The window is half open. He puts the kitten on the windowsill and starts admonishing it:

"*Not* down there, kitty!"

Gregory climbs up on a chair to be closer to the kitten and, still playing with it, pushes it toward the abyss.

"Well, well little kitty . . . go on, little kitty, go on!" Gregory warbles as the horrified kitten loses its balance.

Unaware of the danger, he clambers onto the sill himself to see what has happened to his living toy. Fortunately enough, cats have great coordination, and this little one has managed to land on a windowsill on the floor below without any apparent damage to itself. Gregory looks totally enchanted by his exploits; he remains precariously balanced on the windowsill in order to talk to his kitten, which is desperately meowing down below.

At the foot of the building a number of passersby have stopped in consternation and remain standing there, their faces turned up toward the ninth floor window in which Gregory is perching. Literally petrified by the terrifying situation, they do not dare make a move or shout.

In the meantime, Nicole has arrived on the third floor. She exchanges a few words with Lydie who has gone back to work, repainting the entrance hall of the apartment blue.

"I'm really mad, I can't find my change purse."

"Are you sure you didn't leave it here?"

"Oh no! I don't think I had it anymore when I came in here. No, I must have left it downstairs or in the grocery store, I just don't know."

Nicole descends the stairs.

Now there are at least a dozen persons standing there, holding their breath, staring at the window and Gregory.

What was bound to happen happens: bending over a little farther, Gregory loses his balance and falls.

With one great outcry the passers-by rush toward the child, believing him dead. But Gregory has landed in a privet hedge and bounced onto the lawn, and now he gets up, smiling, and declares:

"Gregory go boom."

Nicole, coming out of the building, has heard the shouts; she arrives on the scene, running, at the moment Gregory gets up, and realizing what has happened, collapses in a faint. Now everybody congregates around the young woman in order to revive her, while Gregory nearby imperturbably amuses himself by kicking an old rusty colander around.

That evening in the still disheveled Richet apartment there is still talk about the day's dramatic events. Jean-François is busy polishing a copper trumpet, lovingly giving it a high sheen, and talking to Lydie who is preparing dinner in the kitchen.

"You know, what really gets me is that everybody just stood around without trying to do anything."

Lydie appears in the kitchen door and replies:

"Yes, but what would you have wanted them to do? They were all looking at little Gregory up there on the windowsill, holding their breath, but what *could* they have done?"

Lydie sets the plates on an overturned crate, covered with newspaper in lieu of a tablecloth. Her husband helps her set the "table," and they sit down.

"What was really unbelievable," Lydie goes on, "was when he landed on the ground. We all rushed to see, thinking the worst had happened, but what do you know? The little one just got up, looked at everybody with a big grin on his face, and do you know what he said? 'Gregory go boom!' "

The young couple laughs, but Jean-François quickly becomes serious again.

"It's just terrifying to think about all the things that can happen to children. I think they're in danger from morning till night."

"Yes . . . well, that isn't entirely true, because if the same thing had happened to a grownup person, well, that would have been it. Children are very sturdy, they go banging against everything, they bang themselves against life, but they are really graceful, and they've got a pretty thick skin, too!" concludes Lydie with a smile that expresses her great confidence in life.

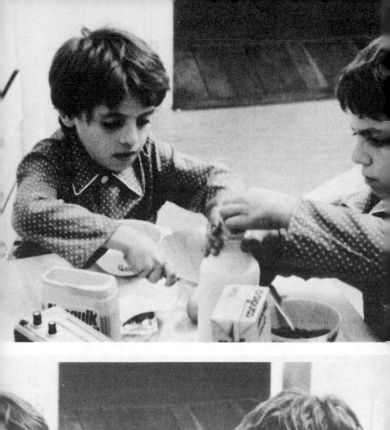

VII

Children Are Bored on Sundays

The courtyard of a somnolent apartment building: some windows are already open, but most of the shutters are still closed. We hear Charles Trenet's pleasant song:

> *Les enfants s'ennuient le dimanche,*
> *Le dimanche les enfants s'ennuient*
> *En knickerbockers ou en robes blanches*
> *Le dimanche les enfants s'ennuient.**

In one of the apartments the Deluca brothers, Mathieu and Franck, are up and about. As Franck goes to open the door to his parents' room, the older brother stops him:

"Leave them alone, it's still early. Come on, let's get breakfast."

In the kitchen the two boys get busy: milk, bread, butter, chocolate, bowls are soon arrayed on the table. At Franck's request Mathieu turns on the television set sitting on top of the refrigerator;

---

* Children are bored on Sundays,
Sundays children are bored.
In knickerbockers or white smocks
Sundays children are bored.

a solemn voice emerges from it, followed by a burst of great organ strains.

"Rats! it's the televised Mass!" says Mathieu and instantly turns it off again.

Franck turns on a little transistor radio and rests his elbows on the windowsill as Charles Trenet's voice resumes:

> *Que ce soient promenades ou tartines,*
> *Pâtissiers pas plus que les bois,*
> *N'auront de succès, gamins et gamines*
> *Sont plus tristes que maman ne croit.**

Mathieu is struggling with the milk bottle, which refuses to open. At last with a determined punch of the thumb he pierces the top and causes the milk to gush forth.

"Oh! Shit, my eye!" Mathieu exclaims, bespattered with milk.

Franck imperturbably butters a slice of bread and urges his brother to do likewise. Then he gulps down a glass of chocolate milk, prepared by himself, and states emphatically:

"Excellent!"

In an empty street Julien pursues his search for who knows what. Now he must have noticed something because he changes tack and crosses the street.

On the other side he walks up to Patrick Desmouceaux, who is working with a rag and a bucket of water on a beautiful but old Mercedes convertible.

---

* Whether it's walks or jam sandwiches,
  Visits to the pastry cook or the woods,
  None of it works, the little boys and girls
  Feel sadder than Mama can imagine.

"Hi there! What are you up to?"

"I'm washing the neighbor's car. I do it every Sunday."

Patrick does not really want to stop working to talk to Julien, who walks around the automobile, examining it.

"Hey, this is a pretty weird old crate."

"It's a vintage model. He's got a lot of others in his garage."

Julien stands in front of the hood. He casts a glance at Patrick to make sure that he cannot be seen—Patrick is washing the rear end of the car—and proceeds to unscrew the radiator ornament while continuing the conversation:

"How much does he pay you for the job?"

"Three francs."

Patrick has not seen it. In one swift motion Julien hides the radiator ornament in his shirt and disappears down a side street, calling back to Patrick:

"Three francs? I'd like to do that . . . If he wants to have those other cars washed . . ."

Jean-François Richet and his wife walk by, greeting Patrick in a friendly fashion before going on their way to a sidewalk café.

At the first table M. Golfier is perusing the newspaper, his son Richard next to him. While Lydie gives Richard a hug, Jean-François pokes a little fun at M. Golfier:

"How are you, M. Golfier? How's it going? Are you picking a winner?"

M. Golfier replies with some conviction:

"No more of that, my dear sir! Not another penny into the state's pocket!"

"Well, that's sensible," the teacher admits, before walking on with his young wife.

A little farther along, the young couple encounters Nicole Felix, who gives Lydie a broad wink and points at the newspaper she is holding in her hand—*La Montagne*. Lydie replies with a little smile of complicity.

Two little girls collecting money for cancer research stop Jean-François and his wife. Jean-François exchanges a couple of coins for a small pin, and Lydie attaches it to his lapel.

Arriving in front of the café, the two girls separate; while the older one goes inside, the younger one proceeds to work the sidewalk tables. A smiling Mme Felix is sitting there, facing a gentleman whom we can only see from the back. She attempts to keep going a conversation that does not seem too animated. The marriage candidate is not exactly a barrel of fun:

"I lost my father when I was thirteen, but I was lucky enough, I still have my mother. If you'd like, I'd like to take you out there to visit, next Sunday . . ."

"Oh, sure . . . So you really like your job?"

"Oh yes, I really love it . . ."

The two collectors have joined forces again and are now standing in front of M. Golfier.

"Monsieur, this is for the search . . . for the battle against cancer."

M. Golfier isn't having any:

"No, not this time. I've already given some!"

The two little girls move on to other targets, while M. Golfier and his son finish their drinks.

On Sundays life certainly moves at a slower pace. It must be around 11:00 A.M., and some inhabitants of Thiers are still fast asleep.

In the same apartment building as the Delucas

but on the other side of the courtyard lives young Sylvie, the one who does not like it to be said that she was born in a garbage can.

When her father comes into her room, Sylvie is still in her nightgown, busy feeding her two goldfish.

"Good morning, Sylvie. Did you sleep well?"

"Yes, Daddy."

"Say, you really take care of your fish, don't you. Do you think they know you?"

Sylvie does not like being treated like a baby, and she hastens to correct any notion that she is one:

"I know *them* all right. This one's called Plic, and that is Ploc."

Unhesitatingly she points out which is which. Her father decides to play along.

"Oh, so the one that's eating right now, that's Ploc?"

"No. That is Plic."

"Then it must be this one that's called Ploc?"

"No, no, it's that one. *This* is Plic."

"But you just told me that was Plic and that the other one over there was Ploc."

"Yes, but they've swum around since then."

Her father, flabbergasted, decides to give up, but not without a parting shot:

"Listen, I just don't understand those fish of yours. Only if you'd paste labels on their backs, I'd be able to tell them apart ... And now, why don't you hurry up and get dressed. We'll have lunch at a restaurant."

At last Sylvie smiles at him.

"We're going to the restaurant? That's class!"

In her room Sylvie is almost ready. She is

wearing a pretty white floral print dress and is busy cleaning her handbag, which is, in fact, an elephant fashioned out of plush material. She dips a brush into the water of the goldfish bowl and scrubs, without much effect, the dirt stains that cover the animal, all the while talking to it softly:

"I have to clean you up a bit. You're really dirty."

A few minutes later Sylvie joins her mother in the living room. Her mother expresses approval of her dress but seems taken aback by the object she is carrying:

"Say, what is *that*?"

"It's my purse."

"That revolting thing is your purse?"

"It is, too, my purse. It's got all my things in it."

"And what are you going to do with it?"

"I'm going to take it along to the restaurant."

Sylvie seems determined to stick to her guns, but her mother gets upset:

"You're going to take that dirty old bag to the restaurant? But have you considered what it might do to the other people's appetites? It just isn't fair to inflict that on them, is it now?"

Sylvie is unshaken in her determination:

"I want to take it with me."

Her mother tries a new tack, attempting an appeal to her vanity:

"Sylvie, you're really such a neat little girl. You mustn't take that bag with you."

Sylvie does not give in.

"I don't care."

Running out of arguments, Sylvie's mother appeals to her husband:

"Jean-Marie! Do you know what your daughter's come up with now? She has decided to take that

dirty old thing to the restaurant. Just look at it!"

The father bends down to look at the old elephant that Sylvie is firmly clutching to her chest. He finds no difficulty in concurring with his wife but tries to use diplomatic arbitration:

"Listen, Sylvie, you don't really want to take that bag to the restaurant. Look, it's covered with stains; it really isn't too nice, is it? Why don't you put it back, and Mama will go and get you a real lady's purse, right? OK, Cathy, go and get a little bag for her."

Sylvie has lost interest in the problem and starts playing with a bullhorn that lies on an armchair. Her father notices:

"Oh, Sylvie, please leave that alone. You know I need it for my job."

The mother returns to the room and motions to her husband to come over.

"You think this'll do the trick?" She asks in a low voice, showing him a little bag made out of red velvet with a gold clasp.

"I'm sure that'll do, no problem," the father says reassuringly.

Sylvie's mother holds out the bag with the smile of a temptress.

"Look, Sylvie, what I found for you. It's one of my purses. Do you like it?"

Sylvie does not even bother to reply. Standing at the other end of the room, she merely shakes her head. Her father tries again:

"Listen, Sylvie, take the purse. I'm sure you can tell that it's much more beautiful than yours, and it really is a grownup lady's purse. When you carry it, they'll think *you* are my wife. Do you want it?"

Once again Sylvie shakes her head. Her father's tone of voice changes:

"Well then, listen to me, Sylvie. It's as simple as that: either you take this purse, or we'll go, your mother and I, to the restaurant and leave you here by yourself."

Calmly Sylvie replies:

"I don't care."

"You don't care? You want to be stubborn? All right."

Sylvie's parents leave the apartment. A second passes . . . and her father's head reappears:

"Sylvie, there's still time to change your mind."

All Sylvie's father can see is his daughter's back and her hair oscillating from right to left. She has chosen this stance to express once and for all that her mind is made up.

"Well, too bad."

And this time he closes the door. Without a moment's hesitation Sylvie walks over to it, turns the key, takes the key out of the lock, and throws it into the fish bowl.

Sylvie's parents walk across the courtyard, determined not to look back once. Sylvie follows their progress through the window; as soon as they have disappeared, she goes to the living room table to pick up the bullhorn her father has told her not to touch.

It is heavy, and she has to use both hands to carry it. But Sylvie obviously knows what she wants to do. She goes to the open window, rests the front end of the bullhorn on the sill, pushes the button that activates the battery, and her little voice, amplified, resounds throughout the courtyard:

"I'm hungry . . . I'm hungry . . . I'm hungry . . ."

One by one the neighboring apartment windows open, and curious faces appear in them. Even the Deluca brothers have heard Sylvie's voice and

opened their window. The Deluca parents join them, and mother Deluca is the first one to call out:

"What are you doing there?"

Sylvie continues her appeal:

"I'm hungry . . . I'm hungry . . ."

A neighbor to her left inquires:

"Where are your parents?"

Sylvie explains:

"They've gone to the restaurant."

M. Deluca:

"They didn't take you along?"

"No, they left me here, and I'm hungry."

The apartment above Sylvie's is inhabited by Thi Loan, a young Vietnamese woman. She too leans out of the window, her daughter and her husband next to her. She tells her husband:

"It's the little girl on the third floor, to the left."

Her husband, who has a stationery and book shop, replies:

"I know her. I sold her some modeling clay."

Sylvie renews her call with full force:

"I'm hungry . . . I'm hungry . . ."

The Deluca brothers, after consulting their parents, make a proposition:

"Come over and eat with us!"

"But I can't, I'm locked in."

The entire courtyard is dumbfounded: how can they leave such a young child all alone? . . . the daughter of a police commissioner . . . and what if something happened? . . . it's a crying shame . . . in any case, we have to get her something to eat. While the grownups continue their excited chatter, the young Delucas have made a decision.

In the kitchen Mathieu fills up a basket with a generous supply of provisions, while Franck is winding up a thick length of rope.

As they go by, their father inspects the basket and removes from it a bottle of wine, which he finds superfluous. The Deluca brothers cross the yard at a good clip, ascend the stairs, reappear in the landing window one floor above Sylvie, and with Thi Loan's assistance and basking in the admiring looks of all the apartment dwellers, they establish a kind of airlift by means of which the basket descends to halt right in front of Sylvie's window.

The little girl takes the basket, thanks her saviors, and sits down in an armchair to partake of lunch, murmuring to herself with unalloyed pleasure:

"Everybody was looking at me, everybody was looking at me . . ."

VIII

Everybody at the Movies

"Children are bored on Sundays"—happily there are the movies! The lobby of the Monaco is teeming with young humanity. Today's television programs can't be too good.

Standing in front of a poster for *The Loves of Zorro*, Julien Leclou seems to be lying in wait. He spots one of his classmates, Fougerie, and intercepts him before he has gotten his ticket:

"Listen, could you get me in?"

"I can't, all I've got is the money for my seat."

Julien shrugs his shoulders at such naiveté and tells Fougerie:

"Don't be so dumb, I know a way. Follow me."

Julien takes Fougerie to an exit door on the other side of the building. They have to go up the steps next to the movie house and turn into a narrow alley on the left.

When they arrive at the door marked Emergency Exit, Julien tells Fougerie what to do:

"You wait for me here; I'll be back in a couple of minutes."

"Where are you going?"

"I'll go get a ticket. Give me your coins."

Reluctantly Fougerie hands over his coins. Julien pockets them and says:

"Now let me have your windbreaker. Come on, you can trust me!"

Fougerie trusts him, yet looks at Julien with certain misgivings as the latter runs down the steps again with *his* money and *his* windbreaker.

At the box office Julien gets a ticket for six francs fifty and goes in.

There are a lot of people in their seats already; Julien follows the usherette, who is none other than Nicole Felix, Gregory's mother, the mother of the little acrobat who went "boom." Nicole seats Julien in one of the front rows, right next to the center aisle.

As soon as she has walked away, Julien spreads his buddy's windbreaker across the back of two seats, thus indicating that they have been taken, and heads toward the toilets.

To get there, one has to go through a door to the right of the screen, then up some steps, and one then arrives exactly on the other side of the emergency exit. Julien gives a shove to the steel-plate door, which can only be opened from the inside, and calls his buddy.

Fougerie appears, and Julien calmly explains what next:

"OK . . . Right by the aisle, in the fifth row or so, your windbreaker's on a seat. Here, don't forget the ticket."

Fougerie takes the ticket; as he is about to go down to his seat, he hesitates a moment and turns to look at Julien, who reassures him:

"I'll join you in five minutes, as soon as the lights go out."

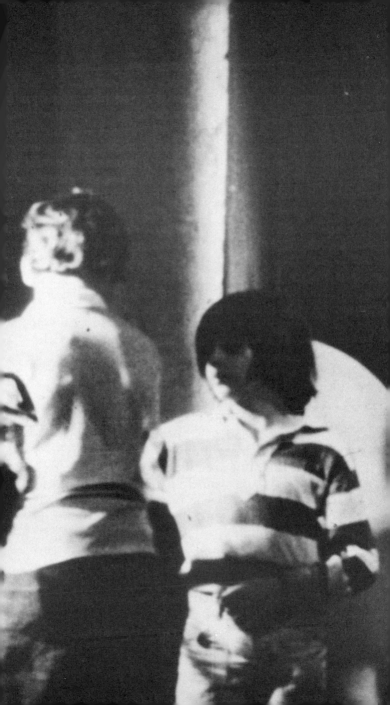

Inside the theater, Fougerie is stopped by the usherette:

"Hello there, young man, where did you come from?"

Fougerie assumes his most innocent expression:

"I'm just coming back from the rest room, madame."

"You have a ticket?"

"Right here . . . and that's my windbreaker, over there on that seat."

Fougerie points at the windbreaker, so astutely placed there by Julien. Nicole, convinced, lets him go. Julien's ruse is working very well.

Now the usherette is leading the Richets to a seat close to the aisle.

"I'll put you here by the aisle, just in case you have to . . ." she says to Lydie, referring to the latter's state of pregnancy.

Lydie touches her arm and asks her in a low voice:

"Tell me, did you meet *the stranger?*"

"Yes, I did. He seems nice enough, but he isn't exactly a gay blade! Every time I laughed he looked around to see if anyone had noticed. So, I guess, not this time around . . ."

The two young women part, and Lydie turns back to her husband, who is curious to know what they were talking about, but Lydie laughs and refuses to tell him.

Toward the middle of the house there are two classmates of Julien Leclou's. One of them, turning around to look, sees something to make him start. He grabs his friend's elbow:

"Hey, do you see, that's Mlle Petit over there . . ."

Both heads turn toward the right. On the other side of the aisle and a little farther back their teacher, in a spring dress, is talking animatedly to a handsome young man sitting next to her.

The other boy is flabbergasted:

"Would you believe it, she's with a guy!"

It looks as if all the inhabitants of the town of Thiers have agreed to congregate at the Monaco today!

In the hallway by the toilets Julien is waiting for the show to start; he hears the strains of the newsreel soundtrack; he gets ready to go in.

In the theatre the lights have gone out. One more time Mme Felix walks down the front row, lighting her way with her flashlight; she has hardly passed the door leading to the toilets when it opens, slowly, and out sneaks Julien, who hurries over to his seat next to Fougerie.

A little farther back Mlle Petit and her "guy" are also looking at the screen, but the young man's hand has a life of its own: it has slowly raised the hem of Mlle Petit's dress, found the juncture of knee and lower thigh, and now rests there, timidly proprietary.

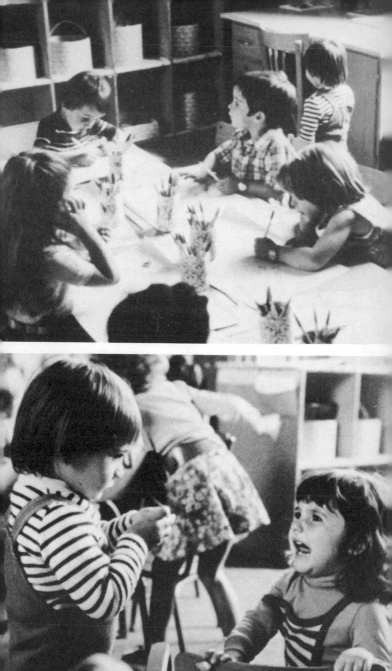

IX

Then There Is the Day Nursery

After singing the song about Sundays, Charles Trenet's voice now indicates the recommencement of the active life:

> *Vienne, vienne la semaine*
> *Lundi, mardi, jeudi.*
> *Car la rue est toujours pleine*
> *De lumière et de bruit.**

Lydie Richet has walked Nicole to the day nursery. Nicole has decided to enroll Gregory there, no doubt hoping to avoid any further perilous acrobatics on his part.

The two young women stop for a moment inside the half-open door and look at the first steps of the infant in this new universe.

Lydie points to a long table around which there are eight to ten youngsters, ages two to four, busy with paper and coloring pencils.

"It looks like a board meeting!"

* Here it comes, here it comes, the working week,
  Monday, Tuesday, Thursday.
  And the street is always full of
  Light and noise.

Nicole is moved by the sight of a little blond fellow with a perfectly round clown's face.

Gregory, inspecting his new domain, passes a group of children around a tub full of water, which they are engaged in splashing around with great glee. Gregory checks out everything—the modeling clay . . . a little girl who is weeping and who elicits a comment from Lydie:

"Yes, some children really get sad, like her. We always think that children are happy, but that's a grownup notion. It really does them good to be among their peers, here. They may cry, but then there's so many things going on that they're soon consoled."

A smiling lady arrives, a little winded, with a big fat blond fellow on her arm; she can hear the other children's voices and laughter and tells her baby:

"I think we're a little late today."

M. Lomay, the gendarme, cannot resist the temptation to stroke the child's nose:

"Oh, but he's such a pretty one! I bet you just love kids, don't you, madame!"

To his surprise, the lady replies emphatically, yet with a stunning smile:

"Kids? I'm positively horrified by them! I know lots of people who just adore children, but I find them really aggravating. I just don't have the patience. They always do what they're told not to do. The only reason I deal with them is because it's my job!"

And she proceeds to carry the child to the classroom, leaving M. Lomay nonplussed. He says to himself, "Well, at least that lady has the courage of her convictions," and goes on attending to his beat.

X

Patrick Looks for Love

At the Desmouceaux' house Patrick opens the window before starting out for school; passing the clock, he notices that it is high time. As always, his father is installed in his wheelchair behind a special little table on which rests a special cup, designed for his handicap. Patrick has gone to check the coffee he is making in the kitchen.

"Just give me the coffee, I can take care of the rest," his father says.

Patrick returns with the coffee pot, pours the piping-hot coffee into the cup, and goes to get his schoolbag and his windbreaker.

"Do you have your sandwich for lunch?" his father wants to know as Patrick is about to open and close the door behind him.

"Yes, Daddy, I do have it."

"Well, good. See you, Patrick."

Patrick has already left.

In the street he hurries because he wants to pick up a classmate on the way. He goes into an elegant beauty salon, and there at the cash register is Mme Riffle, young Laurent's mother, who greets him with a big smile:

"Good morning, Patrick. How are you? You've

come to get Laurent? Wait, I'll call him."

Mme Riffle goes into the hallway next door to the salon, from which a staircase leads to the floor above. She calls out:

"Laurent! Laurent! Hurry up, your friend is here already! You'll be late."

Laurent calls back from upstairs:

"I'm coming! It's just that my hot chocolate is *too* hot!"

"Why don't you pour it into a bowl, that'll cool it off."

While Mme Riffle is talking to Laurent, Patrick stands grinning at a display card on top of the cash register praising the qualities of a brand of after-shave.

Mme Riffle goes back into the salon. She feels sympathy for Patrick, knowing his family circumstances: his mother is dead, he lives with his invalid father. She also likes him for tutoring Laurent, whose mathematical talent is negligible. Mme Riffle surprises Patrick laughing to himself:

"Laurent will be down in a minute. What do you find so amusing?"

"That 'after-shave of M. Seguin's'; I think it's hilarious. Maybe I'll get some for my father, for next Father's Day."

"That's a nice idea. Tell me, how is your dad? He doesn't get too bored?"

"Oh no, now he can read all day . . . he's bought a machine that turns the pages for him automatically."

"That's just great. You'll excuse me, I have to arrange things a bit before opening the place."

Mme Riffle has gone to the rear of the salon, and Patrick remains alone for a moment. He starts daydreaming, looking at a poster advertising sleep-

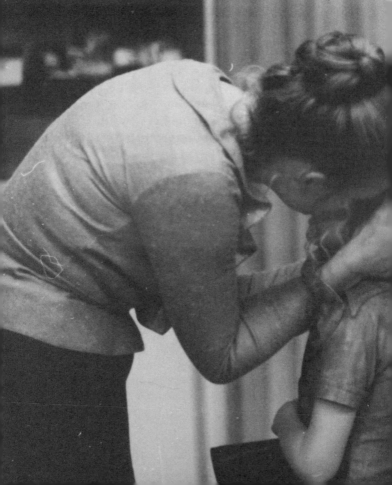

ing cars on trains. We see a compartment and in it
a ravishing young woman wearing a satin nightgown, standing next to the berths; she is smiling at
a pajamaed gentleman in the upper berth,
stretched out with a book by his side and a
cigarette between his fingers. Through the compartment window one sees a night sky brilliant
with thousands of stars. To scrutinize the poster is
to experience a romantic adventure. Small wonder,
then, that Patrick, turning his gaze on the beautiful lady hairdresser, sees Mme Riffle as an appari-
tion gliding through the salon, arranging flowers in
vases.

Patrick is roused from his ecstasy by the arrival
of Fatima and Corinne, the salon's two young
employees. And here comes Mme Riffle again,
pushing Laurent ahead of her.

The boys have hardly cleared the door when
Mme Riffle calls:

"Laurent, haven't you forgotten something?"

Without great enthusiasm, Laurent retraces his
steps and submits to his mother's kiss. Patrick
stands watching with a look that is more dreamy
than envious, a look that is certainly eloquent.

There are many ways of thinking about love; and
who is there who does not think about it?

From within the schoolyard, leaning against the
handrail that demarcates the space of the toilets
close to the entrance, a group of boys, among them
Laurent and Patrick, watch the other pupils arrive.

One mother, while kissing her little boy return-
ing to school, has to bend over the top of the
stroller in which a baby is sitting. This mother is
wearing a fairly short skirt and is thus presenting a

generous view of her thighs and even her underwear.

The boys are watching, giggling and joking, even Laurent Riffle finds this much more entertaining than his mother's kisses:

"Hey! Look, did you see that? It's the full moon in plain daylight!"

By an open window the two teachers survey the schoolyard, while engaged in the discussion of a delicate pedagogical problem. In Mlle Petit's case trouble always starts during the geography lesson:

"There's always two of them in the back of the class playing with themselves all the time . . ."

Jean-François Richet appears to regard that information as somewhat less than tragic:

"Well, you know, that's always been part of the tradition of the secular and public school system . . ."

"As a matter of fact, I think they do it just to provoke me, because I am a woman . . ."

"Oh no, let me tell you, that isn't it at all. I have exactly the same thing going on—but in my case during the history lessons!"

Both of them laugh. Behind them in the yard the boys continue their harmless games, and their behavior seems to diminish the magnitude of the problem that is bothering Mlle Petit. Jean-François Richet, true to his conciliatory temper, goes on reassuring his colleague:

"Sometimes I ask myself if they aren't having contests! You know, since the district only had enough funds to buy six new books at the beginning of this year, I have had to seat them two by two, sharing books . . . I've noticed it a lot of times, but I think it's just part of growing up."

Mlle Petit is still perplexed.

"What I can't make up my mind about is, should I go on pretending that I don't see anything or should I do something about it? I just don't know . . . And should I talk to them individually or address them all together?"

"Do what you feel is right. I only had a real problem once: there was one kid, older than the others, who was a bit of an exhibitionist. So I took him aside during recess and we talked, everything was all right after that."

Mlle Petit gives in a little:

"And you know, it's the same thing with the girls! At Lyons I had a class of girls, about two years ago, and we had exactly the same problem."

"Well, there you are . . ."

"And the school's going coeducational anyway, next year."

"Right, and then there'll be other problems. My brother-in-law teaches a class that's become co-ed, and he tells me the boys have practically regressed back to childhood—they're so intimidated by the girls. Yes, that'll be a different story. . ."

That very moment young Franck in a corner of the yard is the center of attraction for a bunch of boys to whom he is trying to tell a dirty story; he is laughing so hard himself that if they didn't all know it already, none of them would be able to understand a word. Yet through all the giggles and hiccups it is nevertheless possible to guess at the story of Tolitoto:

"You see, Tolitoto's mom tells him to go buy a banana and two lemons. So off he goes, he has to cross a bridge, and he starts back to the house again, but he's lost the two lemons and the banana—he's dropped them off the bridge. So then

the nun comes by, and she says, 'Why are you crying? What's the matter, Tolitoto?' 'I dropped my two little lemons and my banana into the river.' 'Just wait a minute,' says the nun, 'I'll go and get them.' So she jumps in the water. Then the priest comes by, and he too wants to know: 'What's the matter, Tolitoto?' 'I dropped my two lemons and my banana in the river.' So the priest jumps in too . . . And, yeah, they both take off all their clothes before they jump in. And then, in the water, the nun . . . she grabs the priest's banana, and the priest, he gets hold of the nun's two little lemons . . ."

Franck is laughing so hard that he decides to end the story there, saying:

"That's all, folks, that's the story!"

It is also the end of recess. They all file back to the classrooms.

While the pupils are getting into their seats, Mlle Petit walks around the classroom, trying to calm them down:

"Well then, hurry up! Sit down. Silence, please!"

The class has hardly settled down when she starts the lesson:

"Open your grammar books to page 94—page 87 for those of you who have the old edition."

She is now standing in the rear of the classroom next to Julien Leclou, who is the only one who has not taken out his grammar.

"Well, Leclou, aren't you going to get your book?"

"I don't have it."

"You left it at home?"

No answer.

"Where is your book?"

"I don't know. I don't care."

"You don't care, do you? If that's the case, you'll have to spend the grammar study period out in the hall. Go on!"

Without any sign of embarrassment or rebellion, Julien Leclou gets up and leaves the classroom as the lesson begins.

In the hall one can hear M. Richet's class of young ones doing a choral recitation of the multiplication tables.

Leclou proceeds to conduct a methodical investigation of the articles of clothing some pupils have left on the coatracks; he knows there won't be much of any value—old pieces of candy, a dirty comb, some small change . . . He hears a noise and hurries over to the wall, then stands leaning against it, assuming a nonchalant air.

XI

*One Haircut,
Frontier Style*

In the street Patrick encounters Julien, who is
lugging two shopping bags full of wine bottles.
Julien looks morose, and Patrick tries, awkwardly,
to express his sympathy:

"Tell me Julien, did you have trouble with your
folks at home?"

"Leave me alone, goddamn it!" Julien says
brusquely and walks on without even turning to
look back.

An hour later we find Julien in the street again,
playing a strange and dangerous game: standing on
the sidewalk, he stretches out his foot every time
an automobile drives by, as if trying to get the foot
crushed, causing a number of motorists to step on
their brakes.

The Deluca brothers arrive to put an end to
that:

"Come on, let's go—we're on our way to sell
some books," Mathieu tells him.

Right after entering the store, the three boys fall
into a trance of admiration in front of a magnif-
icent compass in a case, enthroned on a display
table next to the cash register. Mathieu decides to
inquire:

"Boy, is that ever a beautiful compass! How much is it?

"Two hundred and fifty francs," replies the store owner, who is none other than Roland, the husband of the young Vietnamese woman, Thi Loan.

"Two hundred fifty francs . . .? Is that *old* ones?" Mathieu asks, hopefully.

"No, that would be twenty-five *thousand* old francs," says Roland.

"There aren't any smaller ones, less expensive ones?"

"Ones like that but not as expensive," Franck specifies.

"Listen, kids, twenty-five thousand old francs is what that one is."

Julien cuts in:

"Why don't you ask your dad to buy you one for Christmas?"

But Mathieu is a realist:

"Not even for Christmas . . . That's too expensive."

Julien makes an abrupt decision:

"Listen, you guys, I'll wait for you outside, OK?"

Julien leaves, and the store owner gets a little impatient:

"So what is it you boys want?"

Mathieu tears himself away from the cased compass, opens his schoolbag, and returns to the initial purpose of the visit to the store. He takes out three used textbooks.

"I came to sell these textbooks. I don't need them anymore, they're old ones . . ."

"But these are this year's books! Won't you still need them?"

"No, I won't . . . I'm moving up a grade, and we won't have the same books next year."

"What about your brother, then?" He looks at Franck. "How old are you?"

"Ten, m'sieur."

"Ten . . . So, well, he'll be able to use them next year. You shouldn't sell them."

"But we won't be using the same books, monsieur," Franck insists.

The store owner remains adamant:

"Listen, I won't buy any textbooks without a note from your parents! Do you have a note?"

"No, we don't," Mathieu admits.

Franck does not give in so easily:

"And what if someone doesn't *have* any parents?"

"All children have someone who is responsible for them! There always is someone."

It is obvious that the storekeeper is not going to change his mind, and Mathieu and Franck realize they won't be able to make the transaction. Deeply disappointed, they leave the store.

In the street they are intercepted by Julien, who has been waiting a little farther on:

"I've been waiting for you," he says and raises the hem of his tattered jersey, revealing what he has been concealing under it—the wonderful cased compass.

Franck and Mathieu are dumbfounded. They had no idea that their buddy had walked off with it.

"I know what I'm doing," Julien remarks laconically.

"How about a swap?" asks Mathieu.

But Julien has made up his mind:

"No, I want some money; I'm going to sell it."

Mathieu's and Franck's attention is diverted by the appearance of Richard Golfier, and while

Julien goes off on his own, the Delucas corner Richard.

Mathieu speaks first:

"Hey, listen, I want to ask you something. You wouldn't have a ten you could lend us ... until Monday?"

Richard says he doesn't.

Mathieu prods him:

"You don't have it, or you don't want to let us have it?"

"I've got eight francs, but my father gave them to me to go and get a haircut."

Mathieu's face brightens.

"To go and get a haircut?"

He smiles to himself, repeating the phrase:

". . . go and get a haircut . . ."

Next we see the Delucas and Richard Golfier in the basement of a nearby building. Richard is sitting on an old overturned crate, some kind of dirty old dishcloth round his neck and shoulders, and Mathieu and Franck, armed with large slightly rusty scissors, are ready to provide him with the haircut he requires; their first decision concerns the division of labor. Mathieu makes it:

"All right, I'll cut one side, and you do the other."

Richard, who is looking a little doubtful, gives them a final piece of advice:

"My father's told me that when you get a good haircut, you don't *look* as if you'd been to the barber."

Mathieu reassures him:

"Don't you worry; you won't look as if you'd been to the barber."

The Delucas proceed to administer the frontier-style haircut, not without some squabbles and occasional hard words.

Richard, growing more and more alarmed, tries to make himself heard:

"Hey, you guys, don't go so fast! Watch out for the ears! And try to get both sides even."

Franck and Mathieu go on cutting with determination and delight, up to the moment when, as they stop to contemplate their handiwork, the two barbers realize that they have managed to make their client look like Attila the Hun ... Richard does not see them exchange a look of dismay above his head.

An hour later Jean-François and Lydie Richet, emerging from the elevator on their landing, are surprised to hear raised voices in the Golfier apartment. It is mainly Richard's father's voice that is heard:

"But that is incredible! You can't throw money out the window like that! No, Richard. It's too late to cry now; come on, let's go! And don't be too surprised if I tell you that I'll cut off your allowance for a month."

The apartment door is flung open and M. Golfier appears, dragging Richard.

M. Golfier returns the young couple's greeting in a curt manner, swearing under his breath as the elevator doors close in front of his nose; still holding on to his son, he rushes down the stairs, turning for a moment to shout to Jean-François Richet:

"By God, I don't know how you do it, dealing with *thirty* of them! But he hasn't heard the last of it!"

At the Riffles' beauty salon and barbershop, there is only one male client to whom M. Riffle is

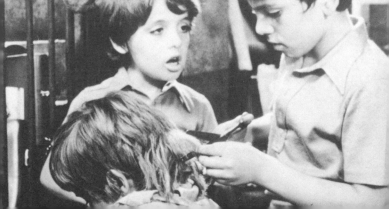

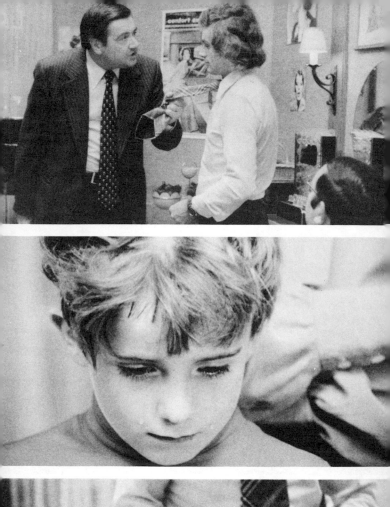
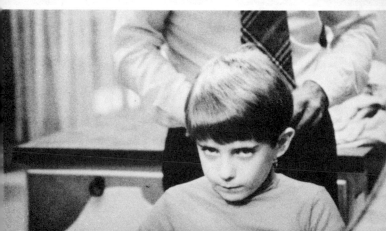

applying the finishing touches.

"Do you want your hair parted, Monsieur Lomay?" he asks.

M. Lomay comes back with one of his jokes:

"Hell, no! Divided they fall!"

Both men laugh. Mme Riffle is getting ready to lock up after her two employees leave as M. Golfier bursts in, followed by the hapless Richard. Mme Riffle tries to stop him:

"No, no, no. It's too late, we're closing . . ."

But nothing and nobody can halt M. Golfier, whose face is a choleric purple.

"I haven't come to get a haircut, I've come to ask your husband for an apology!"

M. Golfier orders Richard to wait by the door and hurtles toward M. Riffle.

"Yessir, apologize! It's a scandal, that's what it is! There are things you just can't get away with. I want you to explain what happend to my son's hair!"

M. Riffle retains his composure.

"That's no way to come in here, you know. If you've got something to say, please calm down and say it. We aren't savages here."

In the apartment of the Riffles right above the salon Patrick Desmouceaux and Laurent Riffle, busy with their homework, hear the noise of the fracas below. They hurry downstairs to find out what is going on.

From the hallway they can take in the entire scene at a glance—Richard, blushing and hanging a shaggy head which Mme Riffle is contemplating with a perplexed expression; M. Golfier, purple with rage, despite his own words:

"But I *am* calm, I'm *perfectly* calm . . . I've simply come to ask you what it is you've done to my boy here! This morning I gave him money to go and have his hair cut . . . and now look at him!"

M. Riffle, braving the storm:

"Listen, Monsieur Golfier, for four years running I've won the hairdressers' gold medal . . . How can you believe that I'd be capable of such a massacre?"

Now Richard, tears in his eyes, has to confess the truth.

Ten minutes later Richard, sitting in one of the barber chairs, looks a little more cheerful. M. Riffle has skillfully repaired the damage done by the Deluca brothers, and M. Golfier is both calmer and ashamed for his previous choleric behavior.

"He looks quite a bit more presentable. Do forgive me, but, you know, when I saw him come home looking the way he did . . ."

M. Riffle feels generous:

"No, no . . . No reason to . . . I would have felt the same way."

"How much do I owe you?"

M. Riffle has his modest moment of triumph:

"Nothing at all, I won't take your money . . . not a penny! I've done it for the sake of the good name of us barbers!"

When M. Riffle returns to his apartment, Patrick and Laurent are just finishing up their homework on the dining room table. Mme Riffle comes out of the kitchen, carrying a stack of plates. She asks her husband:

"Well, did M. Golfier calm down, finally?"

"Yes, he did . . . It all turned out all right. He even wanted to pay me, but I refused, of course!"

M. Riffle goes and sits down in his armchair and opens the newspaper while his wife starts setting the table. The two boys are stowing away their

books and notebooks; Laurent's mother turns to Patrick, with a sunny smile:

"Why don't you stay and have dinner with us?"

"My father's waiting for me back home."

"Well, but you can always give him a call. What do you think about that, Ernest?" Mme Riffle asks her husband, who raises his eyes from the paper long enough to remark that he thinks it is a good idea.

In his small apartment Patrick's father sits reading. It takes only a light touch on a lever to activate the mechanism that turns the pages of his book. His reading is interrupted by the ringing of the telephone. With his one somewhat functional arm he sets the wheelchair in motion and steers it toward the telephone; it isn't far.

The telephone is also equipped with a special mechanism; the receiver is attached to a metal bracket at the level of M. Desmouceaux's face, and all he has to do is to stop in front of it and press a button with his forearm to take the call.

M. Desmouceaux sounds pleased to hear Mme Riffle and immediately agrees to her having Patrick stay over for dinner. It is obvious that Patrick's father has arranged everything so that he can get by in spite of his handicap and that he is glad to permit his son to lead a life that is almost as normal as that of other children.

At the Riffles the evening meal has begun. It is a hearty dinner, and Patrick does it justice; he has two helpings of pot roast, eats his salad with gusto, accepts three different kinds of cheese, two pieces of fruit, and receives the gateau with a big smile.

After dinner Mme Riffle walks Patrick to the door downstairs. As he is leaving, the youngster, who wants to act like a "man of the world," ceremoniously declares to the young woman:

"Au revoir, madame, and I thank you very much for the frugal repast."

Nadine Riffle finds it hard to control her urge to laugh until the door closes behind him. She switches off the light and goes upstairs to bed.

XII

The Next Sunday the Children Are Not So Bored

From his window Patrick Desmouceaux's father exchanges a friendly smile with the movie house projectionist, whose booth is just across the street. We can hear the soundtrack of the movie being shown, and Patrick's father seems to be pleased by what he hears, because he turns his head toward the interior of the apartment and says:

"Patrick, I think it's a good movie they're showing this week, you should go!"

Waiting for the next performance to begin, Patrick and Bruno Rouillard, who is still basking in the prestige he earned by his dramatic interpretation of the miser Harpagon, amble through the vacant streets of the town past the display windows of closed stores.

Even in demand on request programs, Charles Trenet's radio voice once again pours forth from the open windows:

> *A travers les rues, sans rien dire,*
> *On parcourt la ville sans fin.*

*Y'a qu'les mannequins qui font des sourires
Aux vitrines des grands magasins* *

In the center of town Julien Leclou is walking about, alone as ever. A man he does not know walks up to him.

"Listen, young man, how would you like to make five francs?"

Sure Julien would like to, but what is it he would have to do? The man explains:

"You see the house over there? You go up to the third floor, the door on the left. You ring the bell, and then you give this note to the lady—if it *is* a lady who comes to the door."

"And if it's a man?"

"Just tell him that you made a mistake, that you're on the wrong floor."

Julien agrees. He pockets the money, takes the note, and walks over to the building.

On the third floor he hesitates for a moment and performs a mental check on "left" and "right" before ringing the correct doorbell.

It takes a few seconds for the door to open on a plump brunette with curly hair. She is holding a jam sandwich in her hand and has to swallow a bite before talking.

"What is it?"

"A gentleman I met in the street asked me to give you this message."

"A gentleman?"

"That's right," says Julien and holds out the note.

The woman casts a glance over her shoulder and

* Down the streets, without a word,
  They endlessly walk through the town.
  Only the manikins are smiling
  In the windows of the department stores.

then takes the note, quickly stuffing it into her pocket, thanks Julien, and closes the door. Are the adults, too, getting bored on Sundays?

Patrick and Bruno have stopped in a square, in front of a movie poster. What is it they are waiting for? Suddenly Bruno's face lights up:

"She's nice, that one there. Too bad she's all by herself."

Patrick looks in the direction of Bruno's stare and sees a pretty brunette, at least thirteen and a half years old, who is crossing the square. She hesitates and turns to look at them before going into one of the buildings. Patrick feels obliged to say:

"Listen, why don't you go on, I'll see you later."

Bruno won't have it:

"Out of the question, we stick together."

The girl has disappeared, in any case. But now Bruno makes another sighting:

"Hey, look at that! Let's go!"

Patrick always finds a good reason to restrain himself:

"But listen, are you crazy? Look, there's three of them!"

"So what?"

"There's only two of us!"

Too late. The three girls walk away, laughing, and our two wolf cubs remain in front of the movie poster advertising *The Temple of the White Elephant*.

Ten minutes later two girls arrive on the scene, one taller than the other; this time Bruno pays no heed to Patrick's misgivings.

"Wait for me here!" he says.

And off he goes.

Patrick watches his buddy intercept the girls,

talk to them for a few seconds, and then wave for him to come over.

Patrick goes, as there is nothing else he can do now. Bruno, very much at ease, introduces his classmate to the girls: Corinne, a brunette of fourteen or so, who is even a little taller than Bruno, and Patricia, blonde and smaller—even so, Patrick is obviously impressed by her—it is the first time he has picked up a girl.

At the box office Corinne bethinks herself once more as Bruno is about to get the tickets:

"Listen, Bruno. I have to think about this. I'm not so sure I want to see the movie."

"Come on, that's no fair—you just said you wanted to see it."

"Just let me think a minute. Let me talk to my friend."

And there are further murmurs between the two girls while the boys stand waiting by the box office.

But it all works out, and the two young wolves and their conquests are seated in the balcony of the Monaco. Their seating order is: Corinne, Bruno, Patrick, and Patricia. Patrick is the first to strike up a conversation:

"Is that your sister?" he wants to know, nodding in the direction of Corinne.

"No, that's not my sister. She just lives across the street from us."

The conversation comes to a halt. Bruno, on the other hand, tries a more direct approach. Corinne is too young to be tackled with the classic "Do you live with your parents?" but Bruno has no difficulty in finding an equivalent:

"What grade are you in?"

Corinne has a peculiar habit. At regular intervals she pulls at the collar of her sweater, lowers her head, and casts a look inside, as if to make sure her young breasts are still there. She raises her head again to reply:

"Oh, I'm leaving school. I want to become a beautician."

The lights go out, and the theme music of the Pathé-Journal newsreel cuts off their budding conversation. The narrator's opulent voice fills the house, while newsreel shots fill the screen. The show is on.

This week, our first story is about the star everybody is talking about: Oscar! Yes, Oscar, going from one triumph to the next on the stage of the Européen! Every night after his performance all of Paris tries to crowd into Oscar's dressing room, but it takes more than that to make him stop whistling.

On the screen we see a music hall dressing room; a pan to a mob of photographers and reporters; then the arrival of a white-faced Pierrot in traditional costume, who goes and sits down in front of the mirror of his dressing table.

This is followed by shots of the liberation of France as the narrator continues:

Oscar was born thirty-one years ago, in 1945, right after the war.

The year before that, in August 1944, Madeleine Doinel, a young Parisian girl, nineteen years old to be exact, had gone like thousands of other young women to greet the American troops, who were expelling the invader from our country.

In the atmosphere of patriotic joy and general festivity that was characteristic of the Liberation, Madeleine, Oscar's future mother, found herself in the middle of the night and of a heavy flirtation with Peter Nicholson, a GI from Kentucky.

The images of cheering crowds have been superseded by others of a more intimate nature—couples of amorously intertwined GIs and young Frenchwomen disappearing into the shrubbery.

In the arbors of our public parks there were quite a number of little Frenchwomen that night, learning to masticate the chewing gum in the arms of their liberators.

As is often the case, the nature of the images on the screen stimulates the audacity of the couples in the audience. Thus there is a definite flurry of amorous activity in the theater. Bruno has first of all put his hand on Corinne's shoulder. Then he leans over and kisses her. Patrick has observed Bruno's action but hesitates to try anything with Patricia, probably because he finds her too young. Yet Patricia is casting glances at her friend, who is in full erotic swing.

On the screen we now see images illustrating the marriage of Oscar's mother to the GI. The narration drones on:

For Madeleine Doinel the flirtation proved to be a serious one, and nine months later Oscar was born.

The "international" marriage ceremony took place just in time. The bride wore white, but the gown had to be of a rather ample cut to allow for the roundness of her figure.

The Nicholsons got along very well, although Madeleine found it very difficult to learn to speak English, and Peter never succeeded in learning French.

In the theater Patrick gathers up his courage and turns toward Patricia. Before he has had time to do whatever it was he intended, Patricia, after glancing once again at Corinne and Bruno who are still locked in an embrace, hisses at him:

"Such idiots!"

Patrick, discouraged, sinks back into his seat, telling himself that he was right not to try anything with Patricia. He docs not know that a girl of her age is quite likely to say the opposite of what she thinks, the opposite of what she wishes.

On the screen we now see Oscar as a baby in his cot, working on his bottle.

The narration goes on:

What effects would this drama of communication have on Oscar's development? Would his first words be English or French, or would the hesitation between those two lead him to rediscover instinctively the languages of his ancestors, Latin or Hebrew? Well, the baby's choice was a really unpredictable one. Unable to pronounce a single word, he chose to express himself by whistling.

And, in fact, baby Oscar, whose bottle is empty, now starts banging it with his hand and *whistling* to attract the attention of his parents.

Oscar was no instant virtuoso, but with the help of a few tremolos he was well able to make his parents understand that the soup was too salty . . . And if they did not respond to his calls with sufficient alacrity, he was liable to get violent.

Oscar is now sitting in a high chair. He is whistling and pushing his soup plate away with a disgusted mien; since no one shows up, he takes the full plate and throws it on the floor.

Then we see Oscar at the age of two, in the sandpit with a small female friend of the same age:

With a few trills that are just as eloquent as words Oscar manages to persuade little Marion that her toys belong to him, too.

Oscar at ten, dressed in the traditional first

communion outfit, whistling next to a young girl communicant, who is crying:

Older but not wiser, Oscar obstinately refused to kiss his cousin on the day of their first communion. It is said that she was so mortified that she kept her veil and entered a convent.

In the theater Corinne and Bruno, their arms around each other, cast sideways glances at Patrick and Patricia and realize that the situation of the other couple is not improving. Corinne whispers a few words in Bruno's ear, and Bruno nods vigorously and turns to Patrick in order to whisper in his ear.

The story of Oscar continues; we see him as an adult, dressed in the Pierrot costume:

Today, in 1976, Oscar is thirty-one years old. He still does not talk but has succeeded in transforming his handicap into a prestigious and remunerative stage act. Here he is on the stage of the Européen.

In the balcony we see the result of the whispered conferences: Bruno and Patrick change places, and we now have from left to right Corinne, Patrick, Bruno, and Patricia. This means that Bruno and Corinne have agreed to change partners out of the kindness of their hearts, in order to encourage Patrick to abandon his position of neutrality.

While this is going on, Oscar's story draws to a conclusion:

Oscar's story is positive proof that it is quite pointless to run after things—you just have to whistle for them.

And the narrator's voice moves on:

Our next story takes us on a cruise in the Caribbean.

As Raymond Queneau has remarked, "The doc-

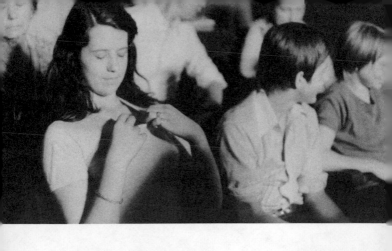

umentary isn't it / The kids, they think it's shit."
But our young couples have no intention of
watching this one, even with half an eye.

While the narration of the voyage to the
Caribbean drones on about the perennial colorful
crowd and its doings, the events taking place
between our four protagonists in the balcony are
far more interesting. Without wasting time or
scruples, Bruno has proceeded to fondle Patricia,
who is a willing partner and does not seem to find
it idiotic at all. But Corinne and Patrick have
reached an impasse. Is Patrick intimidated by the
size of his lady? Does he feel squeamish because
she was lying in his buddy's arms only two minutes
ago? In any case, he stares straight ahead at the
screen, indifferent to the encouraging glances Corinne is casting in his direction. She, too, seems to
be looking at the screen, but her eyes are in fact
turned sideways like those on an ancient Egyptian
frieze; while she does not have any inhibitions
against necking, she still adheres to the tradition
according to which it is up to the boy to take the
first step.

After a moment, during which nothing has
changed, Bruno and Patricia, who have been
observing the other two between kisses, get up and
motion to Patrick to change places again. The
third rearrangement results in this new order, still
from left to right, Corinne, Bruno, Patricia, and
Patrick at the end of the row—yes, Patrick, whom
the three accomplices regard with a touch of pity—
and Bruno, dedicated as ever, puts his arms around
both the girls and smiles now at one, now at the
other.

Patrick, excluded from the game of love by his
own choice, Patrick whose feelings cannot be

fathomed, sits up very straight in his seat, staring at the screen in resignation; but who is he trying to convince that he finds the demagogic claptrap of a documentary, patriotic to the point of debility, more interesting than the charms of his female companions?

XIII

A Child Is Born

It is dark, totally dark. We hear the sound of someone knocking at a door, and a rectangle of light opens up onto an apartment where everyone is asleep. It is the middle of the night. Now M. Golfier appears in the hall, tying the belt of his bathrobe, heading for the door as the knocking continues.

"All right, all right."

As soon as he opens the door, Jean-François Richet dashes in. He is so excited that he can hardly talk.

"Monsieur Golfier! Oh . . . excuse me . . . it's my wife, she . . . she's about to give birth . . . so . . . so I have to call the hospital immediately. Your phone . . . where is it?"

M. Golfier leads the teacher into a room and switches the light on.

Mme Golfier appears in the hall.

"What's happening?"

"It's that young Lydie, she's in labor. Go and look after her, will you?"

Mme Golfier hurries toward the Richets' apartment.

Young Richard, roused by the noise, is on his

feet now; he has opened the door of his room and tries to figure out what is happening—the lights being switched on, the shadows flitting through the hall, the whispered conversation; all of it makes him feel like a character in a thriller.

M. Golfier crosses the hall, disappears into another room where the light goes on, reappears carrying a telephone directory, and goes back to M. Richet, who is babbling into the phone.

"Hello ... Hello ... but what *are* they doing, I just can't believe it ... a maternity hospital that doesn't answer ..."

Finally the father-to-be seems to have succeeded in waking someone up and in explaining the situation:

"Hello ... Yes, listen, this is the Jean-Zay Apartments, Building E ... Yes, right, we need an ambulance, my wife is in labor ... Yes ... no ... but you will be there, won't you, we're counting on you ... Yes, we'll be downstairs in just a moment."

Mme Golfier comes back, supporting Lydie who has slipped a raincoat over her nightgown. She is carrying her little hospital suitcase. Through the half-open door Richard watches them leave, his eyes round and wide.

In the hospital's delivery room M. Richet stands holding his father's old Rolleiflex, ready to take pictures of the birth of his child. But then, in spite of all his resolution, when the moment arrives and the nurse tells him to proceed, he is paralyzed by emotion. The nurse has seen this happen before: "Come on now, if you want to take pictures, this is the time to do it." But Jean-François suddenly looks like a little boy again, and his wide-eyed expression is very similar to Richard's.

The following morning, in the corner of the schoolyard where the latrines are, Mathieu Deluca is engaged in conspiratorial activity: he takes two very realistic-looking toy revolvers out of his bag and hands them to two friends, who hurry to conceal them inside their shirts and hurry off without further ado.

Entering the classroom, M. Richet's pupils take possession of it with much noise, seeing that their teacher is not there yet. The school janitor, M. Touly, comes to put an end to the racket:

"Quiet, children! Your teacher will be a little late this morning. Now be reasonable, don't make me climb those stairs again."

He has hardly closed the door behind him when one of the pupils announces:

"*I* know why he isn't here this morning."

"Why?"

"Because his wife's had a baby."

Mathieu Deluca knows even more.

"Yes, and he's even taken pictures while his wife was giving birth!"

This calls forth loud exclamations from all sides of the classroom.

"What for? To sell them?"

"What a swine he must be!"

Mathieu explains:

"No, no, they're pictures of the baby!"

The center of interest shifts radically:

"What is it, is it a boy or a girl?" one of them wants to know.

Everybody ventures a guess, but little Franck has the last word with his stunningly precise opinion:

"It's twins, nonidentical ones! If they don't know if it's a boy or a girl, it's got to be twins!"

The teacher arrives to put an end to all the

speculation. He's a strange-looking teacher this morning; he obviously hasn't shaved, and he looks tired, happy, and excited all at once.

"Good morning, boys . . . sit down. Well, as you see, I'm late . . . Today is a special day—I have a child."

Now they know their curiosity will be satisfied.

"Is it a girl or a boy?"

"It's a boy."

Renewed outcries of joy.

"What's his name?"

"Thomas! His name is Thomas."

And the happy father picks up a piece of chalk and writes it in large block letters on the blackboard: THOMAS.

A small voice from the back of the class:

"Thomas, as in to-mah-to."

Richard Golfier has risen to inquire:

"And how is your wife?"

The teacher replies with a big smile:

"She is all right. She is tired, you know, but she is very happy."

The questions come tumbling:

"Does he have hair? . . . How big is he?"

"Fifty-one centimeters," the young father announces proudly.

"And how *wide* is he?" asks Richard, who is a stickler for precision.

"Ah, that I can't tell you."

"Are you going to bring him here?"

The teacher smiles:

"Well, he's got to grow a little, you know."

"How much does he weigh?" another pupil wants to know.

"Three kilos and three hundred grams!"

The precise figure causes a murmur of admiration.

M. Richet says:

"Well, all I want to tell you, today, is that . . . that I'm very happy."

He decides not to put on his gray smock after all, throws it on the desk:

"Won't need this today! Let's make this an open session, I didn't have time to prepare anything."

He reflects for a moment—then:

"This morning we'll practice oral expression . . . Richard Golfier, stand up."

Richard stands up.

"Well, tell us how you spent your Sunday."

Richard begins, without enthusiasm:

"All right . . . I got up late . . . I slept a lot . . ."

He lapses into silence. M. Richet tries to make him go on:

"And then?"

Richard draws a deep breath and continues:

"I slept a lot, I got up late."

M. Richet can't help smiling:

"Well, it doesn't seem like you're too interested in telling us about what you did on Sunday."

Richard, who has been hanging his head, raises it again:

"Can I talk about motorcycles?"

M. Richet is not about to refuse any request today:

"About motorcycles, all right. Go on, but speak out so that we can all hear you."

Richard starts talking with the confident voice of someone who knows what he is talking about:

"There are a number of different makes; there is the Suzuki, the Gus Kuhn, the Triumph, the BSI, the BMW, the Kawasaki, the Peugeot . . ."

Off to a good start, he is unfortunately interrupted by a discreet knock on the door. It opens.

It is M. Berbert, the principal, followed by a scowling gentleman who is none other than the father of the Deluca brothers.

All the boys have gotten up. The principal tells them to sit down and asks M. Richet to come out into the hall. For quite a while the three adults talk in low voices, now and again casting a glance into the classroom where tension is mounting; everybody is wondering what has happened, and the Deluca brothers look even more anxious than their classmates, possibly because they *do* know. Finally M. Richet addresses the class:

"Listen boys, I am told that the Deluca brothers have given some of you some toys. That was very generous of them, but those toy guns do not belong to them—or rather, they've been bought with money that wasn't rightly theirs."

While talking, the teacher has walked to the back of the class. He turns around and concludes his speech with an emphatic gesture:

"All right, now it's your turn. Let's have them back!"

One after the other more than half the pupils raise the tops of their desks and hurry toward the teacher's desk, jostling each other, to cover it in a big pile of revolvers.

XIV

Patrick Makes His Move

This evening, as on many others, Patrick has come to the Riffles to tutor young Laurent—this time it is the new math.

But Patrick does not seem to have all of his mind or all of his heart on the job, and Laurent has to call his young tutor back to reality time and again, as he sits dreamily staring at a photograph of the beautiful Mme Riffle.

Within the hour Patrick has decided to take action. Standing in a small square of the town, he hesitates only a moment before striding over to the florist's shop on the other side of the street.

Once inside he states that he wants to make a gift of some flowers but does not really know what kind.

The florist is helpful:

"A gift? Well, why don't you get some roses."

Patrick raises his head to look at the sign the florist is pointing at and reads:

"White roses . . . tender love."

"Pink roses . . . secret love."

"Red roses . . . ardent love."

Patrick decides quickly:

"I think I want some red roses."

He hands over two fistfuls of change, which indicate the patience and the time it has taken to get the amount together.

Patrick hurries down the street. He is not too far from the Riffles' barbershop and beauty salon. He walks faster, casts a look into the salon, then recoils quickly to hide in the entrace hall of a building next door. Who is he hiding from? It's only his buddy Laurent who emerges, almost immediately, from the salon. Patrick watches him walk away, and as soon as he has receded, Patrick leaves his hiding place and advances once again toward the salon. He is acting like a burglar: instead of walking into the salon, he chooses the door next to it, the one that leads to the hallway giving direct access to the apartment. In the hall Patrick stops for a second, long enough to take a look at the interior of the salon and to make sure that M. Riffle is there with the two employees and a couple of customers.

Then he proceeds up the spiral staircase to the apartment. Halfway up he stops again, in the manner of someone on a diving board; he overcomes that final hesitation and goes on.

In the apartment the beautiful Mme Riffle is sitting in front of a mirror applying nail polish. She is so engrossed in this that Patrick has to clear his throat before she notices his presence. She turns toward him with a big smile:

"Oh, it's you, Patrick? How are you? You better hurry if you want to catch up with Laurent, he just went out."

Patrick takes the plunge. Looking straight into Mme Riffle's eyes, he says:

"I haven't come to see Laurent, madame, I've come to see you."

"Me?" Mme Riffle says, surprised.

Patrick's self-confidence crumbles a little and he develops a slight stammer:

"Well yes, I thought ... I want to ... Well, here," handing her the bouquet, "this is for you."

"For me? Oh, but that's nice! My, they're beautiful! Oh, I'm so pleased!"

Mme Riffle takes the roses, looks at them, sniffs them with genuine pleasure. Deeply moved, Patrick is ready for anything, except for what she says next.

"Make sure to thank your father for me!"

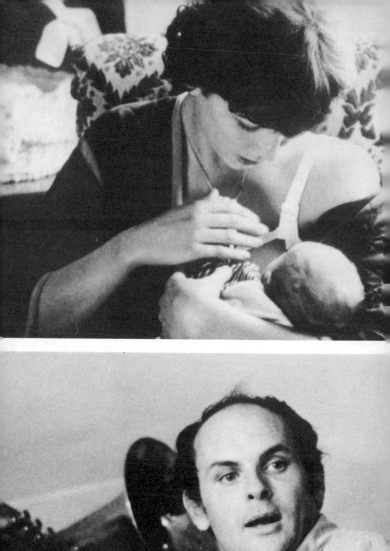

XV

Theory and Practice

The new baby has arrived in the Richets' apartment.

Lydie is breast-feeding him. Standing on a stepladder, her husband is arranging his books on the shelves; he has stopped to turn the pages of a book. He can't resist the temptation to read to his wife a passage that strikes him as of particular interest and whose author, Bruno Bettelheim, is a specialist in childhood matters:

"While breast-feeding, the infant is well aware whether he is being held in an anxious or a realxed manner. It is not simply a question of comfort. The infant's wellbeing or unease will influence his entire future behavior, and his later relationships with women will depend directly on his initial relationship with his mother."

The young mother has listened to the "lesson" her husband has read to her with an ironical smile, while the baby has been sucking avidly, leaning snugly against her arm. She looks up at Jean-François and says, laughing:

"Your relationship with your mother must have been a pretty good one!"

A little later the baby is back in his crib. Richard

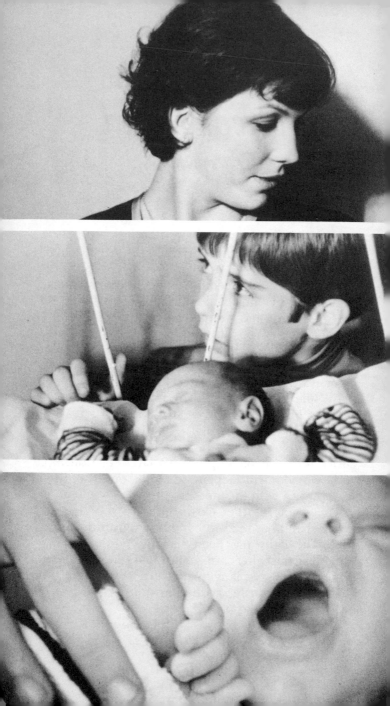

Golfier has come to see him and is now kneeling by the crib and gently stroking the little face with one finger, all the while firing questions to which Lydie is patiently replying:

"How many days old is he now?"

"Well, it must be fourteen days tomorrow. You remember? He was born on a Sunday night."

Richard has not forgotten:

"That's right! And in the middle of the night, too!"

He watches the baby for a moment.

"Sometimes I think he's smiling at me."

"Really? But, you know, babies don't really start smiling until they are at least a month old."

"That may be, but I've seen him . . . he smiled at me! Do you leave him alone all the time?"

Lydie reassures him:

"Oh no, I'm busy with him all the time, as you can see."

Richard strokes the miniscule ear with his fingertips.

"He's got such nicely formed ears!"

Now the baby wakes up and clutches Richard's hand.

"He's holding on to my finger, he won't let go!"

"That's right, all babies do that. They grab hold of things and really hold on to them."

Richard has one final question:

"When will he be bigger?"

"Oh, I don't know. Perhaps tomorrow."

XVI

Julien in Revolt

A heavy rain is falling on the town. Julien Leclou, holding his schoolbag over his head with both hands, is rushing up the wooden staircase leading to his home.

He goes in, but only a moment later the door opens and he reemerges, evidently propelled out with some force.

In the doorway stands his mother, her hair tousled, her clothes shabby, yelling at him:

"If this is when you come home, you can go to hell! I'll get by by myself, as always."

She closes the door of the shack.

In a rage Julien picks up a large rock and hurls it at the door, breaking one of the glass panes; then he runs off, without waiting for the reaction.

Night has fallen. Julien, wandering aimlessly through the streets, arrives at a fun fair.

He gets rid of his schoolbag by slipping it under the ticket booth of one of the merry-go-rounds. Now he can walk around without attracting attention. All around him there are lights, happy squeals, the tempting spiels of the carnies; but as he probably does not have penny in his pocket, he has to content himself with just looking at it all.

Walking by a neighborhood bistro, Julien casts a mechanical glance inside: there are a number of hookers in there, and also Bruno Rouillard who is negotiating with one of them at the bar. She is examining his school ID:

"Come on now, stop kidding me ... 1962, it says; you're fourteen."

"But I've *told* you that I am sixteen," Bruno insists. "I erased the date just so I could still get half rates at the canteen. Just look at the date: it's been scratched!"

"No, no, it won't do," says the girl haughtily. "Try one of the others; I won't do it."

In the dawn's gray light we see the boats, carriages, bicycles of the merry-go-rounds covered up in their sheets of canvas. Julien, who has passed the night in the streets, returns to get his schoolbag from its hiding place.

He stays there a little while, gets up on the platform of the airplane merry-go-round, and picks up items that have fallen out of the pickets of last night's revelers; he finds an old comb, an empty cigar case, a nail file, and even a couple of coins.

An hour later M. Touly, the janitor, opens the gate to the schoolyard as he does every morning. He is surprised to find young Julien sleeping in front of the gate, curled up on the sidewalk.

"Well, it's you, Leclou! What are you doing here? Have you been sleeping here? School only starts in an hour."

He helps the boy to his feet.

"You're really dirty. Come on, let's get you cleaned up a little."

And the good man leads the boy across the yard. A little later that morning Mlle Petit is in the

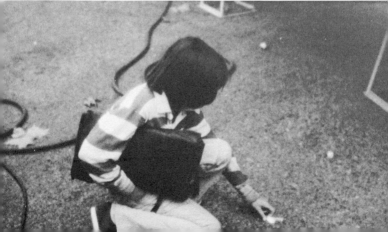

process of dictating to her class when the janitor knocks at the door:

"Good morning, mademoiselle. I've come to tell the boys that it's time for their medical checkup."

Mlle Petit dismisses the class:

"All right, boys, get going."

Welcoming any interruption, the pupils file out with smiling faces. Only Julien Leclou remains in his seat, apparently determined to stay there.

But M. Touly has noticed:

"What about you, come on, then."

"My parents told me not to go."

"Do you have a note from them?"

Julien has to admit that he doesn't.

"Well then, come on, everybody else is going!"

Reluctantly Julien gets up and, dragging his feet, follows M. Touly.

In the yard the boys stand in line by the wall, waiting their turn to pass by the doctor. They are all stripped down to their shorts, though a few timid souls have kept their T-shirts on.

Julien joins the line but stands a little apart at the very end.

In the line there is a bit of chatter about that. Bruno and Patrick are already discussing their vacation. Bruno has very definite plans:

"My parents have joined the Club Méditerranée. I'd really rather go back to Arcachon because that's where my girl cousin is . . . and this time I won't be as stupid as I was last year; I won't let the opportunity slip by again."

The janitor, who is trying to keep a semblance of order, has heard the end of that conversation. He asks Patrick:

"What about you, where are you going for your vacation?"

"I'm going to a summer camp, m'sieur."

He adds, with a big grin:

"But it's a coeducational summer camp!"

A commotion at the end of the line attracts the janitor's attention. Some boys have noticed that Julien has not stripped, and they get on his case:

"Hey, listen, Leclou, you have to take your clothes off like everybody else!"

"You've got to take your pants off!"

"Hurry up, do it!"

The shouting gets so loud that the nurse appears in the window of the room where the examination takes place and asks for a little silence. The janitor tells her:

"Mademoiselle, it's a pupil who does not want to undress!"

"All right, bring him in, we'll check him right now!"

And Leclou has to walk down the line, pursued by the wisecracks of his classmates.

In the examination room the doctor and the nurse manage to get Leclou out of his perennial tattered jersey and push him toward the X-ray machine. The room is dark, the only light emanates from the apparatus; the silence is oppressive.

As the boys stand waiting for their turn in the schoolyard, the nurse suddenly appears and runs toward the principal's office; the boys stop talking, aware that something important has happened.

The door is closed, the principal is not there. The nurse turns around, starts running again. M. Richet catches up with her.

"Please help me find the principal!"

"Let's see if he's in the stock room!" M. Richet says, and they hurry toward another door.

Mlle Petit has observed the commotion from her

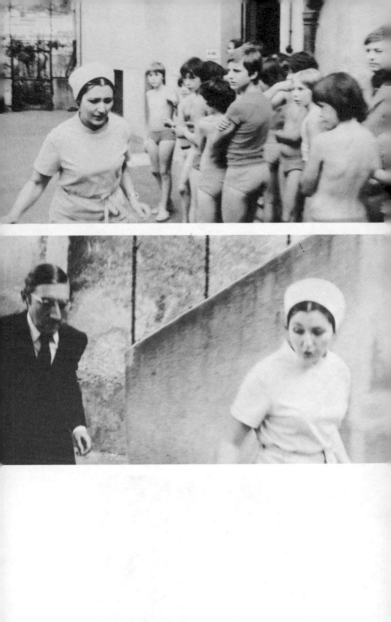

classroom window. She shouts:

"No, no—the principal isn't there, he just went by here. He is next door."

The nurse ascends the steps leading to another door from which M. Berbert emerges:

"What is the matter?"

The nurse does not stop to give lengthy explanations but leads the principal to his office, saying that "it is very urgent, and the doctor wants to see you."

By the office the doctor, a gray-haired woman, stands waiting.

"M. Berbert, this is a very serious matter," she says. "We'll have to call the police commissioner."

They all enter the office. The door closes behind them.

The boys are now standing in a corner of the courtyard with M. Richet and the janitor, who announces:

"Ah! Here he is!"

Preceded by the gendarme, M. Lomay, the police commissioner, enters the yard.

At a brisk pace they proceed to the principal's office where Mlle Petit, the doctor, and the principal himself are waiting.

M. Berbert, always observant of the courtesies, makes the introductions:

"Monsieur Lomay, Dr. Lartigues."

The doctor then tells the commissioner why he has been called:

"This is what happened. We have been conducting the regular medical checkup this morning, and they brought me a child who refused to undress. It turns out that that child is covered with bruises, scars, and burn marks."

"Did you question him? What did he say?" the commissioner wants to know.

"He said what all those children always say: 'I fell down, I bruised myself.'"

"What class is he in?"

The principal gives a concise answer:

"His name is Julien Leclou, and he is in Mlle Petit's class."

The commissioner turns to Mlle Petit:

"And you, you never noticed anything?"

Mlle Petit, too upset to reply, falls back into an armchair and bursts into tears.

XVII

What Was Julien's Secret?

In the Mureaux quarter a group of neighbors huddles in front of Julien's house. The commissioner comes out, and behind him, flanked by gendarmes, two women—Julien's mother and grandmother, wild-haired, startled expressions on their faces, looking like members of some savage tribe.

The gendarmes have to control the curious crowd and even protect the two women against its anger. But Julien's mother is uncowed; handcuffed, she directs a stream of invective at the bystanders.

"Don't look at them, Mother, turn your head the other way! And why don't you get out of here, go home! This is private property! Get the hell out of here, you scum!"

"A bunch of bed wetters!" adds the older woman, who does not appear entirely sane.

"He isn't unhappy, is he, my boy," the mother goes on, eager to justify herself, "he goes to school. Right, Mama, he goes to school, doesn't he?"

Now they have reached the police van. Julien's mother hides her face behind an old suitcase tied up with string to avoid having her picture taken by the reporter of *La Montagne*.

The commissioner manages to get everybody into the van, and it drives off, pursued by the neighbors' angry yells. One man is so engrossed in the lynching spirit that he runs after the van for a few meters, shaking his fist at the two "child butchers"—the French expression which, curiously enough, has no feminine counterpart.

This morning everything in the schoolyard seems a little different. First of all, Mlle Petit is all dressed up. She goes over to Jean-François Richet, who also seems less relaxed than usual.

"Listen, Monsieur Richet, if you don't mind, can you take my pupils into your class today? I have to go to the police station to answer their questions."

"Don't you worry, I'll do that," Richet replies.

But Mlle Petit feels the need to confide in somebody:

"This business with Julien . . . you know, I can't sleep nights anymore. It's all I think about! I reproach myself endlessly, because I just didn't understand, and I was often hard on him."

"But no, no, Chantal, you mustn't blame yourself like that," Jean-François tells her warmly. "You must not confuse the problems . . . and you have to keep in mind that Leclou tried his very best to let nobody know what was going on at home."

In the street a car horn honks twice, and Mlle Petit walks away. Jean-François Richet watches her go, then walks back to the middle of the yard, thoughtfully lighting a cigarette. Looking around, he notices that the pupils appear calmer than usual. They are talking with each other in small groups without expressing any interest in an event that is, after all, momentous: under the janitor's supervision moving men are piling up the old desks from M. Richet's class and carrying in new ones that are far more up-to-date . . .

Recess is over. As he has promised Chantal Petit, the teacher combines both classes.

Thus the room fills with fifty-five pupils, three to a desk, some standing in the back of the class, some sitting on the radiators and windowsills.

Jean-François Richet does not intend to turn this into a run-of-the-mill class period. He is aware of the tension Julien Leclou's story has generated in the children, and he has decided to discuss it openly with them.

He leans on his desk, looking at fifty-five attentive faces, and starts speaking, into the total silence.

"Well, I know that you're all thinking about the same thing, you are all thinking about Julien Leclou; you have read about him in the papers, and your parents at home have been talking about him, with each other or with you.

"Now the vacations are coming, and I too would like to talk to you about Julien. I don't really know much more about Julien than you do, but I would like to give you my point of view.

"First of all, I have been told that Julien is now a ward of the child welfare authorities. He'll be placed in a foster home. Wherever that will be, it will obviously be better for him than staying with his mother and his grandmother, who did not treat him right or, to be frank about it, who abused him. His mother will be declared unfit to take care of him, which means that she loses her rights to decide about his life. I think that Julien will really be free only when he is fifteen or sixteen, free to come and go as he chooses.

"When we hear a story as terrible as Julien's, our first reaction is to compare it with our own. I had a hard childhood, though it was much less tragic and painful than Julien's, and I remember how impa-

tient I was to grow up, because I felt that the grownups had all the rights and that they were able to lead their lives as they wanted. An unhappy adult can always start over, he can move to some other place, he can make a new life for himself. But an unhappy child can't even *dream* of doing that; he knows he is unhappy, but he can't give his unhappiness a name, and as we know, inside himself he can't even really and truly doubt his parents or other adults who are making him suffer.

"An unhappy child, a martyred child, always feels guilty, and that is what is so awful about it.

"Among all the injustices there are in this world, those concerning children are the most unjust, the most ignoble, the most detestable. The world isn't just, nor will it ever be, but we have to go on fighting so that it gets to be more so. It is necessary, we have to do it. Things are moving, but not fast enough; things get better, but not quickly enough. The politicians, the people who are in charge of our lives, always tend to begin their speeches by saying, 'The government won't give in to the threat,' but in actual fact it is just the other way round, it *always* gives in to the threat, and no improvements ever happen unless they are brought about forcefully. For some time now, the grownups have understood this, and they have gone out into the streets to get what they could not get in the offices of the bureaucracy.

"The reason I'm telling you all this is to show you that the adults, whenever they really want to, are able to make their life better.

"But in all those battles the children have been forgotten; there is not one political party that really concerns itself with children—with children like Julien or with children like you—and there is a reason for that: it's because children don't have a vote. If they would give children voting rights, you might ask for more day nurseries, more social assistance, more of whatever, and you would get it because the representatives want your votes. You could, for instance, obtain the right to start school an hour later in the winter instead of having to run there in the dark.

"I also want to tell you that it is because I have bitter memories of my own childhood and because I don't like the way children are being treated that I have chosen this profession, that I've chosen to be a teacher.

"Life is not easy, it is hard, and it is important that you steel yourselves in order to meet it. I'm not telling you to become callous, I am telling you to grow strong.

"By some ironic justice, those who have had a difficult childhood are often better equipped to enter adult life than those who have been very sheltered, very loved; it is a kind of law of compensation.

"Life is hard, but it is also beautiful; why else would we hang on to it the way we do? It's enough to have to stay in bed with the flu or with a broken leg to realize that one wants to be outside, to run around, to realize that one really loves life a whole lot."

The pupils have been listening to their teacher with seriousness and attention. He gets up and starts walking around the desks while talking:

"Now you're all going to go on your vacation, you're going to discover new places, new people, and when you come back, you'll all be in the upper grade. I have to announce that classes will be coeducational next year . . . and then, as you'll see, time is going to pass very quickly—and one day you too will have children. I do hope that you will love them and that they will love you. To tell the truth, they'll love you all right if you love them. And if you do not love them, they will take their love, their affection, their tenderness to other people or to some other thing, because life is arranged so that one cannot get by without loving or being loved.

"Well, then. School is out, boys, and I wish you a happy vacation."

XVIII

The Summer Camp—The Coeducational Summer Camp!

Mérindol summer camp is located in a handsome château surrounded by parkland. Today everybody is out hiking—the girls on one side, the boys on the other, walking at a good clip, flanked by their counselors—and everybody is singing a marching song, if somewhat chaotically:

A kilometer on foot does wear, does wear . . .
A kilometer on foot does wear out one's shoes . . .

Among the many other faces, we recognize that of Patrick Desmouceaux, who seems to be busier smiling than singing. On the girls' side there is one who responds to his smile; it is Martine, the young girl whom we saw mailing the postcard at the beginning of our story.

The kilometers on foot go by, and the exchange of smiles between Martine and Patrick grows more and more calorific.

That night, when all her friends in the dormitory are already fast asleep, Martine is still wide awake.

Sitting up in bed, she is writing to her cousin in the light of her battery-operated flashlight pen:

> Well, here it is, it has happened!
> On the train on our way to summer camp I noticed him immediately. And I saw that he had noticed me, too.

In her mind's eye Martine sees the train again and all the children frantically waving goodbye. In one of the windows stands Patrick, too busy smiling at Martine to participate in the general leave-taking, and she is looking back at him.

Martine returns to her letter and amplifies:

> His name is Patrick. Yesterday we were taken to a track to watch races between bicycles pulled by automobiles. Needless to say, I didn't watch them much . . . nor did he.

She sees again the racetrack and the huge black cars with their drivers standing practically upright and behind each car a bicyclist pedaling like mad. In the grandstand the spectators are numerous and excited. By the curves there are tiers of seats where the summer campers are sitting—the girls on the right, the boys on the left. In the midst of all these heads turning to follow the racers, two faces remain still—those of Martine and Patrick, who are looking at each other.

Martine continues her report:

> Today at noon we were in the refectory, and I was suddenly overcome by a pressing urge.

In the camp's big dining room lunch is just

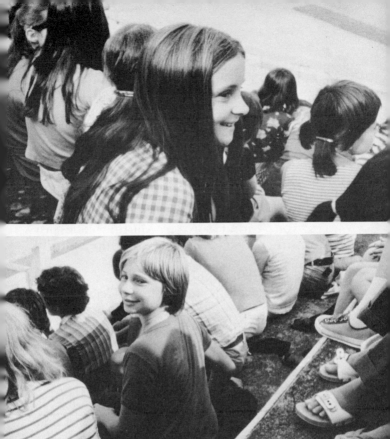

about over. Martine hands an apple to the girl sitting next to her: "Keep it for me, will you? I have to go pee."

She has hardly left when her friends decide to play a trick on Patrick. One of the girls calls out to Patrick, who sits among other boys on the left side of the refectory:

"Patrick! Hey, Patrick!"

Patrick raises his head.

"You talking to me?"

"Yes, you. Didn't you see Martine? She just went out to give you a kiss. So hurry up and find her!"

Patrick is a little embarrassed because his buddies start giggling all around him. He does not want to get up.

But the girl insists:

"Go on! She's waiting for you!"

Patrick hesitates no longer. Courageously he gets up and leaves the dining room, ignoring the other boys' laughter.

In the room next to the dining room there is no one at all. Patrick goes up the grand staircase that leads to the dormitories.

Just as he disappears from sight, Martine, coming from the rest room, is seen at the end of the hall going back into the refectory. She starts heading toward the girls' tables, back to her seat, but a boy calls out:

"Martine, Martine!"

She stops.

"You didn't see Patrick? He went out to give you a kiss!"

Martine does not hesitate at all. She leaves in a hurry.

Up on the second floor Patrick looks into the

girls' dorm: no one there. He checks the boys' dorm: no one there either. Disappointed, he slowly descends the staircase. A slight noise catches his attention; he looks and sees Martine coming toward him.

Very slowly Patrick walks down the stairs to meet her. As they draw closer, they suddenly grow very shy of each other. But Patrick cannot disappoint Martine: awkwardly he takes her in his arms and kisses her, searching for her mouth like a promising novice.

They draw apart again and, in a state of slight turmoil, walk back to the refectory without a word.

They have hardly opened the door to the dining room when they are met by peals of laughter and exclamations from all their camp mates.

As Martine puts it in her letter:

> Was there ever an uproar when we got back to the refectory!

The entire refectory is indeed in an uproar. The great collective clamoring grows even louder as Patrick and Martine walk back to their places. What an incredible noise!

It is not a hostile noise, nor is it particularly friendly; it is just a great noise, an explosion of vital energy. All the shouts and yells of laughter light up a hundred and twenty children's faces, sixty boys, sixty girls, and those faces, all similar, all different, remind one of a Chinese crowd: they are the faces of children who are impatient to lead their lives.